Kristy Docherty

WORKING TOGETHER

a framework for collaborating in complexity

Publisher's Note

Every possible effort has been made to ensure that the information contained in this book is accurate at the time of going to press, and the publishers and authors cannot accept responsibility for any errors or omissions, however caused.

No responsibility for loss or damage occasioned to any person acting, or refraining from action, as a result of the material in this publication can be accepted by the editor, the publisher, or the author.

First edition published in the United Kingdom in 2024 by Ideas for Leaders Publishing, a business of IEDP Ideas for Leaders Ltd.

Apart from any fair dealing for the purposes of research or private study, or criticism or review, as permitted under the Copyright, Design and Patents Act 1988, this publication may only be reproduced, stored or transmitted, in any form or by any means, with the prior permission in writing of the publishers. Enquiries concerning reproduction should be sent to the publishers at the following address:

Ideas for Leaders Publishing
42 Moray Place
Edinburgh
EH3 6BT
www.ideasforleaders.com
info@ideasforleaders.com

ISBN
978-1-915529-30-5 – Paperback
978-1-915529-31-2 – E-book

To Toby for all your support

This book would not have been possible without the participants that took part in my doctoral study and the support of the teams at Collective Leadership for Scotland and Project Lift. Both programmes, supported by the Scottish Government, looked at leadership differently through the advancement of new and creative ways of working.

In addition, I am in the debt of colleagues from The Edinburgh Futures Institute at the University of Edinburgh and The Scottish Prevention Hub who believe in the importance of building strong and trusting relationships.

Finally, I would like to acknowledge all of the people who work across our public service system, from education to housing to justice to health, who are challenging established norms and working tirelessly to create fundamental long-lasting change for the better.

CONTENTS

Chapter 1
Introduction 9

Chapter 2
Methodology 19

Chapter 3
Collaboration and Leadership: What Recent Research Has Shown 37

Chapter 4
The Public Services Context in Scotland 53

Chapter 5
The Transformation of Public Services 69

Chapter 6
The Four Principles of Collective Leadership 87

Chapter 7
How Collective Leadership Is Different 119

Chapter 8
The Benefits of Collective Leadership 135

Chapter 9
The Time Is Now 151

Chapter 10
Conclusion: Advancing Collective Leadership 161

CHAPTER 1

Introduction

Over the past 20 years I have held various roles related to the delivery of public services; my work is consistently based on joint projects in partnerships with local government and other public agencies, as well as the private sector and voluntary and community groups. The goal of these collaborative projects is to reduce inequalities by addressing housing, health, energy and other challenges these communities and citizens face. The ultimate ambition is to create a better environment for those who live within disadvantaged communities. The projects I have been involved in have ranged from housing stock transfers from local authorities to housing associations and 'master planning' new communities across the UK to wind, hydro and solar projects, mitigating the financial risk of mass housing refurbishment, and much more. Completion of these projects could take from twelve months to eight years. Despite the wide variety of the projects, collaboration was at the heart of each: the teams working on the projects were all made up of multi-disciplinary professionals who worked for different organizations in different sectors.

And in many cases, the projects had similar outcomes: they were not often successful in achieving the desired change despite the best efforts and commitment of all involved. The core reason, I found, was the difficulty in making multi-stakeholder collaborations work effectively. Many of the collaborations were marked by clear divisions. Project team members often failed to relate to and empathize with each other and even with the communities in which they worked.

This personal, lived experience of ineffective collaboration inspired me to research solutions to the recurring issues that plague and undermine collaborative partnerships among well-meaning organizations and individuals. I felt such research was vital given the consensus that collaborations are becoming increasingly significant in the context of public services (Stoker 2006).

The outcome of my research is described in this book. It quickly became evident that developing more effective collaborative partnerships required changes in the leadership of collaboration. Leadership after all guides how information and knowledge are shared among partners – that is, how such information, learning and knowledge can be consolidated and moved across functional and organizational boundaries. Boundaryless collaboration is especially salient when these partnerships are addressing intractable and systemic issues.

Surprisingly, as Brookes and Grint (2010) have noted, academic research in the field of collaboration often fails to address leadership characteristics and other aspects that can influence the success of partnerships. One reason, according to Fairhurst et al (2020), is that leadership is difficult to describe in collaborative contexts. Perhaps more importantly, they argue leadership may not be considered relevant when collaborating.

In this book, you will learn how, on the contrary, leadership design and practice is key to successful collaboration. I focus specifically on the concept of collective leadership – the idea that collaborations do not require or accommodate single-individual leadership; instead, they function more effectively under a form of collective leadership in which the participants in the project collectively take the leadership role in guiding the project forward.

This book explores the theoretical genesis and development of collective leadership as the leadership approach best suited for public service collaborations, then shows the real-world application of this leadership approach within the context of major collaborative initiatives in Scotland as well as through the experiences of a panel of Scottish leaders in public services.

The antecedents and development of collective leadership as a solution is presented through a review of past research on collaboration and leadership, especially in the public sector context in which I work, revealing the path to this innovative alternative approach of collective leadership. I will show that the growth of collaboration as an incontrovertible requirement for dealing with increasingly complex issues and solutions led to the need for guidance and research on success factors for collaboration.

Focusing on leadership, the traditional, hierarchical decision-making processes on which much of the leadership literature was focused were proving ineffectual, leading to consideration of more distributed and shared forms of leadership. The challenge, however, was how to align practices, assumptions, and goals to achieve leadership that is collaborative but cohesive. The complexity of public services, including the increasing demands placed on them, added to the challenge. Collective leadership emerged as the best approach to meet the challenges and complexity of public service projects and mitigate the frustrations currently felt by many in the public sector.

In Chapter 2, I review the research methodology I used to collect and analyze the data that led to the insights on collaboration and collective leadership presented in this book, which subsequently leads to the Four Principles framework for effectively collaborating within public service contexts.

The connection between the growth of collaboration, the complexity of public services, and the effectiveness of collective leadership is explored in Chapter 3, Collaboration and Collective Leadership.

Chapter 4 dives into the real-world context of collaborative structures of public services in Scotland, including the seminal Collective Leadership for Scotland initiative as well as the work of such organizations as the Scottish Leaders Forum, The Commission on the Future Delivery of Public Services, and Project Lift.

From the macro-level context described in Chapter 4, we move in Chapter 5 to the more micro-level context of the public services pressures as described by a number of public sector leaders who were interviewed for this research. Leaders from local authorities, the National Health Service and the Scottish Government participated in the interviews, which were then analyzed to develop the core themes for a framework of collaboration.

Analyzing the data that emerged from the interviews along with my review of the current academic research, I was able to develop the major themes around which collective leadership could be applied to public services. These themes led to an empirically based framework for collective leadership in public services, presented in Chapter 6, based on four principles:

two attitudinal principles, *inquiry* and *systems,* and two process-related principles, *relationality* and *emergent*, that made such collaborative leadership effective. The Four Principles of Effective Collaboration are shown in Figure 1.1.

The willingness to learn and be open to and curious about different perspectives is essential for collaborations that span organizational and sectoral boundaries, that is an inquiry mindset. A systems mindset, that is, recognizing the interconnectedness of all that happens within the partnership, including how the contributions, processes and outputs from all relevant organizations will impact the outcome, also contributing to the strength of the collaboration. On the process side, members consciously and actively developing relationships with others involved in the collaboration – relationships that go beyond their function in the partnership – will facilitate the collaboration. Perhaps one of the fundamental keys to success, however, is the emergent approach in which experimentation and adaptation drive the project forward as opposed to a more rigidly planned process.

Figure 1.1. The Four Principles of Effective Collaboration

In Chapters 7 and 8, I draw on my interviews with public services leaders to demonstrate the real-world application of the Four Principles. This discussion will cover the major issues that arise with the implementation of a collective leadership approach, including, for example, the changing power dynamics that result from applying the principles.

I will also describe why the Four Principles are effective in the context of public services by describing the change and growth, at the individual and collective level, that result from their successful application. Among the advantages of the Four Principles is a greater ability to recognize the complexity of a problem, the practice of looking at a problem from many different perspectives before seeking a solution, and the vital importance of developing positive, working relationships among collaborators.

Before concluding the book, I explain in Chapter 9 why the time is now for a new approach to leadership in the public service arena. The structural issues, such as silos and organizational walls, and the sensitive relational issues that can arise among collaborators can be mitigated through collective leadership. A recurring theme through the book is the complexity of the issues public organizations face today. Collaborative initiatives strengthened through the power of collective leadership give organizations the best chance of successfully addressing and resolving such issues.

CHAPTER 2

Methodology

Past academic research and my own experiences and familiarity with major Scottish collaborative projects addressing complex social and organizational problems set the context for researching collaborative projects and collective leadership. The next step was to gather through interviews the opinions, thoughts and feelings of public service professionals participating in collaborative projects addressing complex social and organizational problems. These interviews would provide the real-world data that could be analyzed to develop a framework for successful collaboration through collective leadership.

My first decision was to choose the structure of the interviews that would best enable the participants to openly and comprehensively describe their experiences and emotions. My choice fell on semi-structured interviews, which sits between the structured interviews used for quantitative studies and open-ended interviews sometimes favoured for qualitative studies. While the semi-structured interview is also based on a series of open-ended questions, the questions are intended to move the conversation along a pre-determined path so that the discussion remains focused and framed around the topic under investigation (Adams 2015). For each interview, therefore, I had a number of prepared questions that allowed for some flexibility in the conversation but remained consistently relevant to the issues of collaboration and collective leadership. Achieving this balance of focus and flexibility can be a challenge: as a researcher you do not want the participant to stray from the topic, but still encourage them to freely share and provide their insights and reflections.

The key topics for the interview guide I prepared in advance of the planned interviews included defining collective leadership; the practice of collective leadership; and the challenges and prospects of collective leadership. In addition to sharing their beliefs, ideas and experiences around these topics, the participants were asked to provide real-world examples and accounts (Gabriel 2000).

"Authenticity" more than "reliability" is the goal of semi-structured interviews (Seale and Silverman, 1997). Precise dates, for example, are unimportant. More important are the general feelings that thinking about the experience elicits. That is why open-ended 'how' and 'why' questions are so effective, as they typically provoke a more in-depth response. The participants stay on target but still have the space for individual and personal reflections.

Just as the participants are encouraged to openly share their ideas, beliefs, thoughts, and experiences, researchers need to be just as openly receptive in order to 'hear the meaning' behind the responses (Rubin and Rubin, 1995), which extends beyond listening to incorporate the contextual, temporal and cultural inferences that underpin the participants' responses.

Having developed an interview guide, the next step was to choose the participants for the research.

As described in Chapter 4, the Scottish Government had developed the Collective Leadership for Scotland (CLS) initiative. The goal of CLS was to help multi-partner collaborative groups addressing complex service delivery and policy challenges to succeed. The initiative worked with these groups to help them develop the collective leadership required, not only with accomplishing their mandate but also to do so by facilitating the group members' learning and development as they worked on their projects. On average, CLS facilitators worked for six to twelve months (Collective Leadership 2019).

Another Scottish Government programme described in Chapter 4 was Project Lift, which was linked more to an NHS and healthcare setting. All of the participants in our study were connected to and drawn from either the Collective Leadership for Scotland or Project Lift.

Participants for research studies are often selected based on random sampling. That is, the researchers are trying to have a representative sample – for example, the demographic ratios (e.g., 60% women, 40% men) of the sample align with the demographic ratios of the population at large. This study's participants were based on another approach, which is purposive sampling. With this approach, the representativeness sample is less important to the experiences of the participants than that which enables them to offer valuable insight and opinions about collaborating under collective leadership. The participants were not only drawn from the two Scottish Government collaborative initiatives, but were also chosen because they were 1) aware of collective forms of leadership or interested in alternative forms of leadership that rejected the traditional ideas of the individual heroic leaders, 2) enthusiastic about taking part in the study, 3) open to reflecting not only on their experiences with collaboration and leadership but also their experiences with the wider organizational challenges of addressing complex issues, and 4) completely comfortable with taking part in the study and could see no conflict of interest or personal difficulties in doing so.

As shown below, the final list of 20 participants drawn from the CLS and Project Lift initiatives included individuals from various local authorities, the NHS and the Scottish

Government, with a variety of roles, including director, manager, head teacher and psychologist. Whatever their organization or function, every participant wanted to improve collaborative practice by learning more about collective forms of leadership that could better address complex and wicked problems (Heifetz et al. 2009).

Nature of role	Organisation	Participants
Civil Servant (CLS)	Scottish Government	4
Senior Civil Servant (Director Level)	Scottish Government	3
Child Psychologist	Local Authority	1
Organisational Development	Local Authority	1
Head of Finance	Local Authority	1
Educational Manager (Children and Families)	Local Authority	1
Head Teacher	Local Authority	3
Principal Lead (Training and Education)	NHS	1
Emergency Medicine Doctor	NHS	1
Coach/Team Consultant	NHS	2
Programme Manager	Improvement Service	1
CLS Facilitator	University	1
Total		**20**

Table 2.1 – Study data exposure

From March to August 2019, I interviewed twenty participants face-to-face. The interviews lasted sixty to ninety minutes and were digitally recorded and manually transcribed.

Data analysis and interpretation

Once I had the transcriptions, my next task was to analyze them – that is, to define, categorize, theorize, explore, and map the content to yield its learnings. (Bryman and Burgess 2002; Braun and Clarke 2006).

There are, of course, a number of different approaches to analyze data. The approach I selected was thematic analysis, that identifies in the content the major themes that capture an important concept or insight related to the research aim and objectives (Braun and Clarke, 2006). In this case, the impact of collective leaders on the success of collaborative efforts. Thematic analysis is a widely used qualitative analytic method as it is a relatively flexible tool that can be easily adapted to the requirements of many studies while at the same time providing a rich, thorough, and complex interpretation of data.

If there are any concerns with this method, it is the possible role of researchers in skewing or leaning the interpretation of the data because of their own personalities or histories that might lead to bias. This is important because, unlike with a quantitative process, the themes that emerge from the analysis emerge from the reflections of the researcher.

For these reasons, I used a rigorous process based on Braun and Clarke's (2006) framework analysis method of conceptualization, coding, and categorizing the data. This analysis was supported by three software programmes, NVivo, Excel, and MindManager. The goal: to develop an emerging set of constructs and themes that described participants' understandings of collective leadership. The four steps of the analytic process are 1) Transcription and familiarization, 2) Generating initial codes, 3) Code refinement – the search for themes and 4) Identifying key themes (see Figure 2.1)

It is important to note that qualitative data analysis is iterative in nature and the development of patterns and propositions is interactive. Thus, the analysis was not conducted once all of the interviews were completed. Instead, the interviews were being analyzed to some extent as they were occurring, and this analysis could sometimes help guide subsequent interviews.

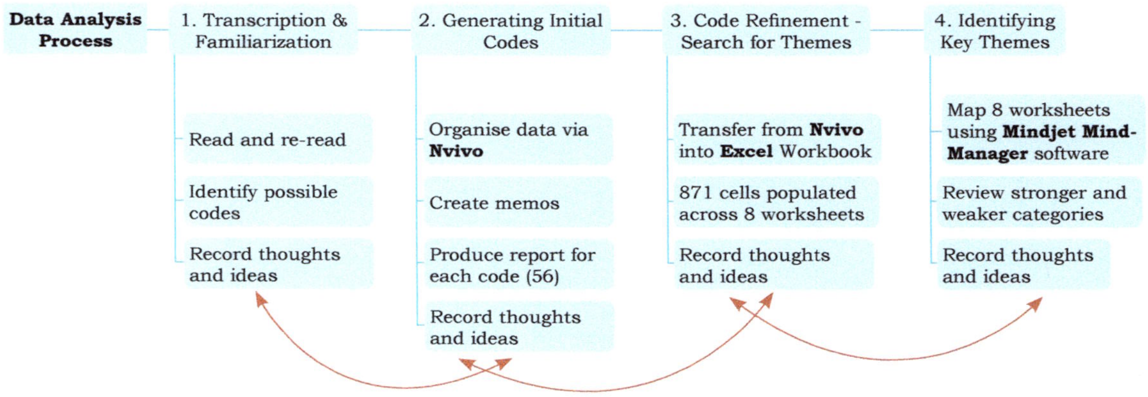

Data Analysis Process

1. Transcription & Familiarization
- Read and re-read
- Identify possible codes
- Record thoughts and ideas

2. Generating Initial Codes
- Organise data via **Nvivo**
- Create memos
- Produce report for each code (56)
- Record thoughts and ideas

3. Code Refinement - Search for Themes
- Transfer from **Nvivo** into **Excel** Workbook
- 871 cells populated across 8 worksheets
- Record thoughts and ideas

4. Identifying Key Themes
- Map 8 worksheets using **Mindjet Mind-Manager** software
- Review stronger and weaker categories
- Record thoughts and ideas

Figure 2.1 – Data analysis overview (qualitative and thematic approach)

As shown in Figure 2.1, once the recorded interviews were transcribed, I read through the transcripts carefully looking for possible codes – tags, if you will, of potential topics or themes that could help organize the insights from the interviews. I recorded some thoughts and ideas and then all the transcripts were uploaded into NVivo, which is a computer-based software program for coding. NVivo is essentially an administrative tool and storage system; and while it can auto-code the interviews by paragraph, it does not analyze the data. It is the researcher's responsibility to analyze the interviews and make decisions and judgments about the ultimate codes or classifications used to organize the research. However, NVivo supports the analytical process, allowing the researcher to monitor how the analysis is conducted and how it changes over time (Woolf and Silver 2017).

Once the data were coded in NVivo, additional software was utilized such as Excel and MindManager – a mind mapping tool that advances the data analysis process and helps the researcher develop initial findings or more developed findings.

Thanks to these tools as well as a rigorous step-by-step analysis approach, I was able to fully immerse myself in the interviews, working with the words of the participants in their many different forms and iterations. Specifically, 1) I listened to what the participants were saying during the interviews, 2) I listened and took notes of their responses during the transcription process, 3) I read through transcripts and recorded ideas, 4) I organized and coded the interviews in NVivo and wrote memos based on my thoughts and impressions, 5) I used NVivo reports to refine the coding and categorizations within Excel and finally, 6) I visualized patterns and developed themes through mind mapping.

The details of the steps taken in my research and analysis, and the timelines involved, are presented in Figure 2.2. By the end of this process, I was fully familiar with the experiences and comments expressed in each interview. More importantly, this thorough process inserted a de facto checks and balances system all during the analysis, so that early ideas and interpretations could be adapted (or rejected) as new information or insights were introduced. This continual comparison of the coded data with the emerging themes maintained and reinforced the consistency and legitimacy of ideas.

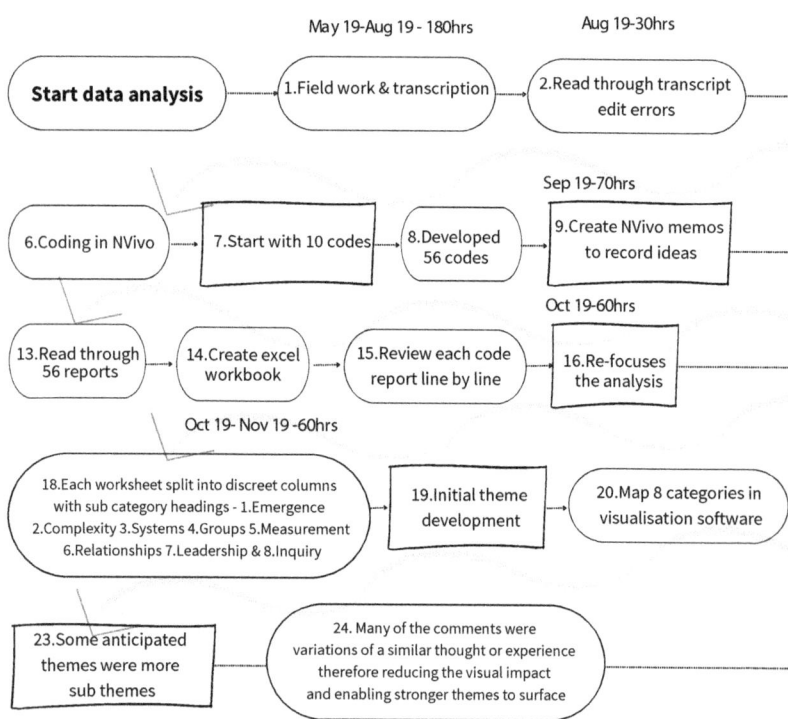

Figure 2.2 – Data analysis and interpretation process

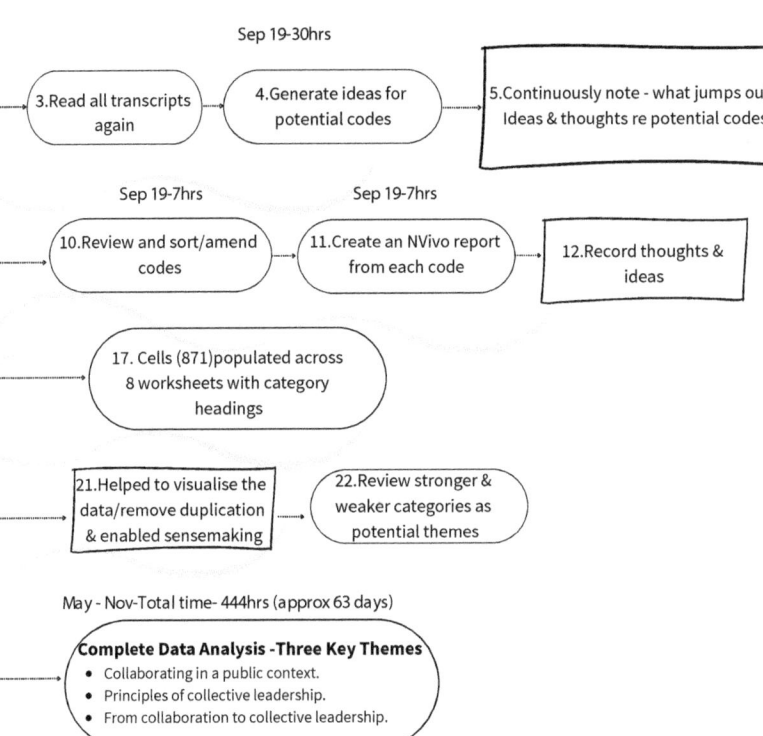

Quality and Rigour

The standing of all forms of research rests on the quality of the methods used. Both quantitative and qualitative methods share a concern that the research itself and the methods of analysis are robust, rigorous and can stand up to scrutiny.

The qualitative interview process in research has been a focus for many scholars, who discuss elements related to interview preparation and staging, the tools and techniques applied, and the different challenges and opportunities associated with collecting and analyzing data (for example, see Alvesson et al. (2017) for an overview). When undertaking qualitative interviews the researcher must be aware of the wider considerations that may impact on what is said and how it is said. Interview accounts can be swayed by place and space (Herzog 2012), gender and power (Aléx and Hammarström 2008) and mutual expectations and assumptions (Potter and Hepburn 2012), as well as hierarchical issues and organizational culture (Silverman 2019). This requires care and thought prior to carrying out interviews and when reviewing and analyzing data.

Schaefer and Alvesson (2020, p. 33) report on their empirical analysis of a sample of interview-based studies where they write extensively about the practices of what they call 'source critique'.

Within this work they discuss the requirement for researchers to take a considered, sensitive and reflective stance toward their data and participants (the source). Furthermore, they comment that a lack of attention regarding the trustworthiness of the data is born out of an overemphasis on the design and coding aspects and that researchers must ask themselves how they are able to justify what is said before making claims and presenting findings. These observations by Schaefer and Alvesson give weight to the views of Potter and Wetherell (1994), Seale and Silverman (1997) and Watson (2009) who question the reliability of interview based qualitative research. Moreover, Barley (2015) states that there is extensive advice on coding in relation to social science research, but less effort dedicated to supporting the authentication and validation of empirical claims.

How can we ensure that the results of our qualitative research and analysis are trustworthy? Lincoln and Guba (1985) identify four concepts that can act as tests of the quality of research results: credibility, transferability, dependability and confirmability. These four criteria can be confirmed through the following questions:

Credibility: Was the data interpreted in a way so that the results genuinely represent the participant experience?

Transferability: Can the findings be generalized or transferred to other contexts or settings?

Dependability: Was the data collection and analytical process carefully documented so that others can follow the steps taken by the researcher and thus able to judge the overall robustness of the work.

Confirmability: Did the researcher take into account their potential biases that they might have introduced into the interpretation? Did they recognize the need to be reflexive and (self) critical about how they viewed the experiences of interviewees?

In my research, I have tried to ensure that the findings are credible, transferable, dependable, and confirmable. For instance, this study is based on interviews with a wide range of people involved in the topic under study but with different backgrounds (professional and personal), perspectives, experiences and interests (e.g. manager, director, vocational role) or representing different corporate and organizational functions. This diversity allows the researcher to review and consider the responses and the meaning behind them and understanding in light of the range of participants and social settings; this also offers opportunities for transferability. Secondly, and as described in the previous paragraphs, the detail provided relating to the study context (Marshall and Rossman 2014), the accuracy of recording and transcribing (Peräkylä 1997), the prolonged immersion into the data (Lofland and Lofland 1995), the multiple iterations of data analysis prior to the final version (Stiles 1993) and provision of an audit trail (Yin 1994) have also been clearly set out within this work to support the transparency, quality and rigour of the research carried out and to offer reassurance as to the trustworthiness of the findings presented.

I also strived to reach the point of *data saturation* – a term that refers to the point where collecting any more data will not elicit any new insights or change any conclusions. In other words, if I had continued to interview more individuals, they would only be repeating the information that I had gathered or opinions and beliefs that I had heard before from previously interviewed participants.

CHAPTER 3

Collaboration and Leadership: What Recent Research Has Shown

A review of past research in the fields of leadership and collaboration which sets the foundation for the insights and discoveries from the research at the heart of this book.

The rise of collaboration

Collaboration is essential for facilitating the work of multiple stakeholders, especially if the project spans organizational boundaries, (Goldsmith and Eggers 2005). Developing public policy and delivering public services require organizations at all levels and branches of government to collaborate on a regular basis, (Poocharoen and Ting 2015). For a number of reasons, however, there has been a notable increase in the popularity of collaboration. One reason is the growing realization that a collaborative approach has a greater chance to resolve challenging issues (DiMaggio and Powell, 1983; Skelcher and Sullivan, 2008). Another reason is that a request for funding from higher levels of government and statutory bodies is more likely to be accepted if collaboration is present.

Both of these reasons point to the same mindset or perspective at the root of collaboration's growing importance in public projects: the issues requiring attention today are difficult for public organizations to resolve satisfactorily because of their complexity, their cost, and/or their scope – many current projects are too far-reaching for a single organization to reasonably and effectively address (O'Leary and Vij 2012; Silvia 2018).

Baggott (2013) draws a similar list of reasons motivating the increase in collaborations within public services. His list includes 1) the push for public service reform, 2) the acknowledgement of systemic issues that cross organizational boundaries, 3) the challenge of managing resources and achieving sustainability and 4) the need to improve outcomes and value for citizens. All have influenced the rise in collaborative endeavours within public services.

Collaborative effectiveness

Organizations are finding they have no choice but to collaborate if they want to address the complex problems challenging today's public services. Decades of research has focused on public service collaboration, exploring the motivation for bringing multiple stakeholders together to resolve complex problems. However, little research has focused specifically on collaboration effectiveness: why some collaborations succeed while others fail to live up to their promise. Taking a closer look at the available research on the 'potential' effectiveness of a collaborative approach offers some explanation for the gap.

Dickinson and Glasby (2010) question the motive for choosing a collaborative approach. They argue that collaborative strategies are not adopted because they are effective, but instead that internal and external factors cause collaboration to be preferred over other options. This preference is reinforced by the assumption that a collaboration will be successful.

Isett et al. (2016) point out that there is limited empirical evidence of collaborative effectiveness. As a result, public leaders base their decisions to pursue collaborations on anecdotal information, organizational benchmarking exercises, or reports of good practice. These leaders thus do not really know whether a collaborative approach is actually working, especially given there is a lack of information on even how to measure collaborative success. Koontz and Thomas (2006) are even more skeptical. Much of the academic debate around collaboration is focused on why collaborative practice has increased, and the difference between collaboration and other approaches – not on collaboration's record of success or even which success factors are required to achieve the desired outcomes.

The core problem, according to Silvia (2018),

is the sheer difficulty of evaluating collaboration due to its inherent complexity: collaborations create a range of different roles, organizations and people, combined with a mix of assumptions, expectations and perspectives. Evaluating collaborative success is as complex as the problems they intend to address.

Collaboration and public leadership

We have reviewed why collaborations are becoming more popular and the difficulty of assessing collaborations. We now bring in the issue of leadership. One of the pioneering studies in public leadership and collaboration was Pedersen and Hartley's (2008) exploration of the changing nature of public leadership in the UK and Denmark. Pedersen and Hartley found that the leadership and traditional operating structures associated with New Public Management (NPM) failed to support the collaboration increasingly required in public service projects. NPM was the term used in the late 1980s for a new focus on the importance of management, quality, and performance in public service delivery. (See Hood (1991, 1995), Dunleavy and Hood (1994) and Pollitt (1990) for detailed accounts of this doctrine.) Pedersen and Hartley (2008, p.327) argued that the "hierarchically organized state" was weakening in the face of diverse stakeholder groups working together across organizational boundaries. In this new, collaborative and networking context, leaders and managers had to adapt their decision-making processes and public service professionals had to adopt specific tools and techniques to manage the tensions arising from both structural and relational pressures.

The weakening of traditional hierarchical leadership was just the beginning. Over time, research in leadership from a public perspective began to chronicle the rise of a more distributed or shared form of leadership. Meijer's (2014) study of police innovation in the Netherlands offers a seminal example of sharing leadership when collaborating. Meijer's study highlights a flatter and more flexible approach to leadership. In this approach all individuals are involved with leadership at different phases in the initiative as it moves up or down hierarchies and across organizations. This perspective of leadership is considered likely to become increasingly important when there are multi-stakeholder groups representing different organizations and where notions of leadership and leading become blurred.

Conditions to support collaboration

As stated above, the effectiveness of collaboration against, for example, an alternative, more centralized approach has not been empirically proven. Past research by numerous authors (e.g. Currie et al. 2011; O'Leary and Vij 2012 and Helms 2016), however, does explore the right conditions that ensures the success of collaborative groups.

Structural and relational challenges and dilemmas must be given special care. How does one address power imbalances? How does one address relational sensitivities, Oborn et al. (2013), given the natural difficulties and tensions that arise between stakeholder groups dealing with complex issues. Leaders recognize that legitimacy and trust are vital to the collaboration's success. Issues of legitimacy and trust, however, are complicated by the unique histories and structures of the various organizations and individuals involved.

The starting point, according to a number of scholars, is a meaningful commitment to the collaborative way of working, this commitment must include efforts to align working practices, processes, assumptions and goals (Himmelman 2001; Thomson and Perry 2006; Selden et al. 2006).

As noted above, Pedersen and Hartley (2008) argued that collaborations required less hierarchy. For Currie et al. (2011) the less hierarchical structure of a collaboration should enable members of the group (as opposed to a single organization) to lead action and change. As a result, with people coming together and working towards common goals, collaborations should be thriving. However, practice does not fulfill the promise of the theory: working with others is less than straightforward and achieving a successful result requires substantial effort.

To help better understand the evolution that collective leadership represents, it helps to review the past 100 years of leadership theory. During this period, the eras of leadership illustrate the context in which leadership scholarship developed. Before 1900, the "great man" perspective of leadership prevailed (and continues to be popular with biographers!). For most of the first half of the 20th century, the great man theory was replaced by the more democratic concept of leadership "traits" – the individual competencies and characteristics that successful leaders shared. The 1940s to 1980s, the "Contingency" era of leadership, witnessed a shift in focus from traits and competencies to leadership behaviours. There are currently two approaches to leadership that have been at the forefront of leadership theory since the 1970s:

transformational leadership, in which the leader offers a vision that transforms the organization; servant leadership, in which the leader is no longer an authority figure who commands followers, but instead a collaborative figure who works with followers. In addition to these two popular concepts of leadership, there are multifaceted approaches to leadership (which also date in the earliest incarnation to the 1970s) that I have grouped into three sets of theories or perspectives: integrated models, critical perspectives, and postmodern perspectives. These three perspectives are explored in Figure 3.1.

100 Years of Leadership

Leader/Follower and Integrated Styles is a move away from the preoccupation with the role of the leader termed 'the romance of leadership' (Meindl et al 1985), these theories tend to revolve around the quality of the leader's relationship with followers, rather than the leader alone.

Critical perspectives are closely linked to the navigation of complexity and uncertainty, and there is a shift by some to move away from traditional, hierarchical, leader-centric models towards a collective, whole-systems approach to relationships and to problem solving (Ospina and Foldy 2015, Fletcher (2012).

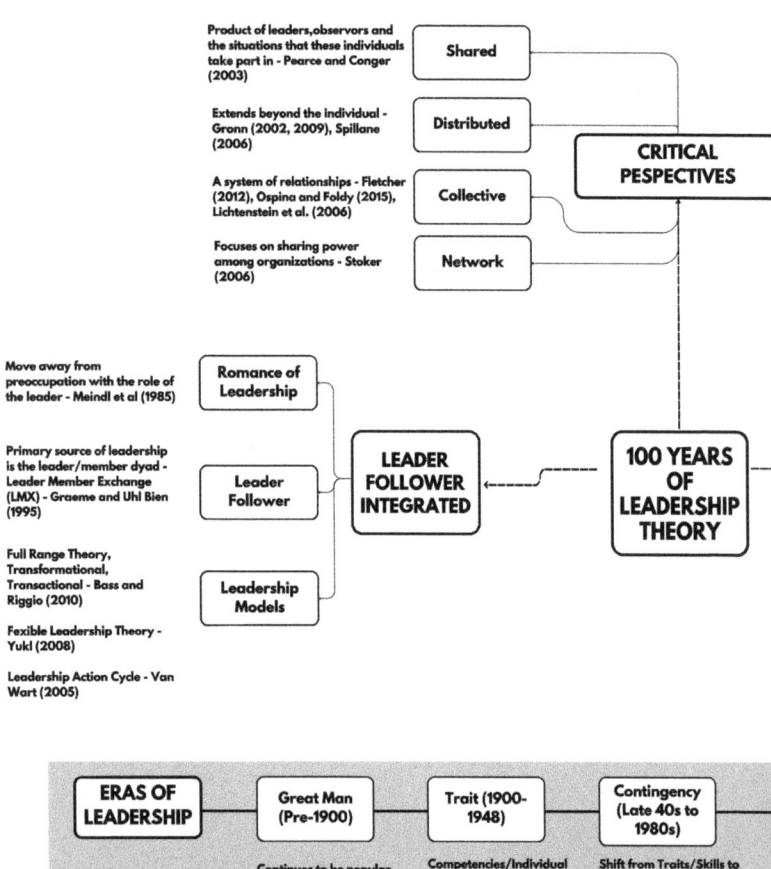

Figure 3.1 Perspectives on leadership

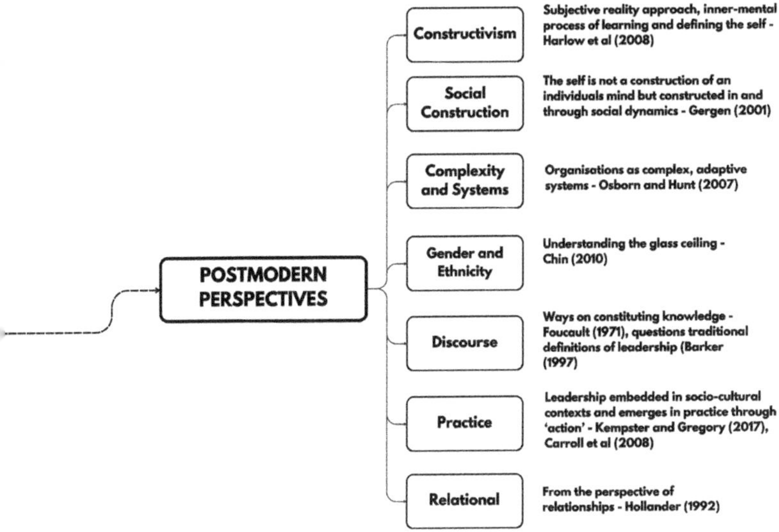

POSTMODERN PERSPECTIVES

- **Constructivism** — Subjective reality approach, inner-mental process of learning and defining the self - Harlow et al (2008)
- **Social Construction** — The self is not a construction of an individuals mind but constructed in and through social dynamics - Gergen (2001)
- **Complexity and Systems** — Organisations as complex, adaptive systems - Osborn and Hunt (2007)
- **Gender and Ethnicity** — Understanding the glass ceiling - Chin (2010)
- **Discourse** — Ways on constituting knowledge - Foucault (1971), questions traditional definitions of leadership (Barker (1997)
- **Practice** — Leadership embedded in socio-cultural contexts and emerges in practice through 'action' - Kempster and Gregory (2017), Carroll et al (2008)
- **Relational** — From the perspective of relationships - Hollander (1992)

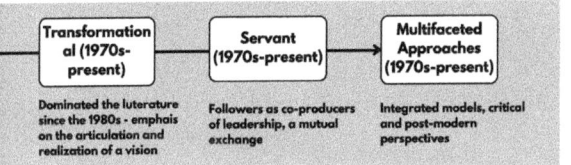

Transformational (1970s-present) — Dominated the luterature since the 1980s - emphais on the articulation and realization of a vision

Servant (1970s-present) — Followers as co-producers of leadership, a mutual exchange

Multifaceted Approaches (1970s-present) — Integrated models, critical and post-modern perspectives

The postmodern perspectives emphasize the diversity of the human experience often defined by gender, background, language, beliefs and values; attention is given to the processes and practice of leadership, and many scholars go beyond entity concepts – a focus on the individual towards groups of people (Gergen 2001).

> Governing has never been easy, but it has become all the more complicated...The process of governing now involves more actors, more policy areas that impinge upon one another, and most importantly involves a wider range of goals.

These words by Peters (2011) capture the complexity-driven challenge of public leadership today.

As Getha-Taylor et al. (2011) explain in more detail, public leadership is leadership with a common purpose and difficult challenges, working across boundaries with and for a range of stakeholders, often with limited budgets and competing ideals. Van Wart (2013, p. 554) describes how in such a context, conventional approaches to overcoming leadership problems are not able to solve public service difficulties (Van Wart, 2013). Public services are distinctive and leadership training will succeed if such training prepared leaders for the "complex set of processes...difficult to perform successfully" that awaits them.

The concept of collective leadership offers an answer since, as defined by Brookes and Grint (2010), public leadership is a form of collective leadership under which different organizations collaborate to achieve a shared vision on shared goals and values. This vision is distributed through each organization in a collegial way. The goal: to promote and deliver improved value to the public – value can be seen and lived in sustained social, environmental and economic well-being – all accomplished within a complex and changing context.

Brookes and Grint's definition conveys the current conditions and environment in which public services must operate. It also provides a somewhat enticing response to how best to deal with complex problems and create public value. But what steps are needed, how can governments go about achieving this 'form of collective leadership'?

One place to start is with the overall result or impact of effective public services, which is, as Brookes and Grint (2010) and other public administration scholars argue, to create public value or better outcomes (Bolden 2011; Meijer 2014; Kellis and Ran 2015; Crosby and Bryson 2018). Delving deeper into these desired outcomes, we find such goals as achieving value for money, delivering continuous, measurable improvement, and managing intense media scrutiny. These objectives reveal the challenge that public service organizations face as they attempt to thrive in an environment that also consists of emerging, complex and ill-defined problems. The goals and objectives referred to, combined with the complexity of the context and issues, present a paradoxical set of circumstances that are difficult, if not impossible to navigate. For interested scholars these demands imply the need to design and embed a collective leadership type of organizational response within public services structures and cultures.

Collective leadership and collaboration

The collective leadership theories developed by scholars are closely linked to the charting of complex and uncertain conditions in pursuit of a shared purpose. These theories offer a different way to think about leadership, applying a collective, whole systems approach to relationships and to problem-solving that replaces the traditional, hierarchical, leader-centric model. Collective leadership is indeed 'collective', meaning that all members of a group and not just one leader have leadership responsibilities. This is a relatively new concept of leadership, and the scholarship in this field is still finding its way. For example, the terminology related to the collective components of this type of leadership is fluid and there are innumerable complementary theories and concepts being advanced that are not clearly distinct from each other or frame the context of collective public leadership in different ways.

Even the definitions of collective leadership presented by scholars, mainly in the last two decades, have been wide-ranging and unfocused (see, for example, Yukl (1999), Friedrich (2009) and Denis et al. (2012) for different interpretations). It is evident that collective leadership is not a straightforward concept to understand, and one can expect the debates and discussions to continue.

Where there is some sort of consensus or shared common perspectives is that the traditional way of working no longer applies in the world of collective leadership, because leadership is no longer about individuals in formal positions; it has become instead a practice, a set of processes and activities applied to make collaborative efforts more effective (Cullen-Lester and Yammarino, 2016). For this practice to be successful, a number of particular skills must be acquired, including deep listening, inquiry, reflection and self-awareness (Gauthier 2015; Sharp 2018). An almost radical new mindset must also be adopted – the mindset that leadership is no longer contained within individuals but is the property of the group and whole system (O'Connor and Quinn 2004). Think of collective leadership as a dynamic process: individuals from across a system come together to form a collaboration, a partnership, or a network, contributing their skills, knowledge and meaning to a shared task (Dansereau and Yammarino 1998; Day et al. 2004). Diversity is the engine that makes this collective leadership work as it takes in knowledge and experiences from a diverse range of individuals – and from these multiple points of view and lived experience flow a stream of innovative ideas and actions that can finally address the complex issues faced by public services in today's environment.

CHAPTER 4

The Public Services Context in Scotland

It was my experiences working in the public service sector in Scotland that inspired the research at the heart of this book – research whose core data, as we saw in Chapter 2, is drawn from the experiences of 20 leaders also working in the context of Scottish public services. Before diving into the details of the pressures and challenges public services face, I want to briefly describe the constitutional and political context in which public service agencies in Scotland operate, and the developing Scottish government network of collaborative and collective leadership organizations and initiatives. The macro-level perspective presented here will help frame the collaborative work featured in following chapters.

The Constitutional and Political Context

In 1999, the UK government devolved to the Scottish Parliament in Edinburgh legislative responsibility for policy related to such matters as health, housing, education and local government. In 2007, the Scottish National Party (SNP) won the parliamentary elections, leading to the installation of Alex Salmond as the SNP's first First Minister. With devolution and the SNP continuing as the party of government in Scotland, the possibility of Scottish independence has continued to be a source of political friction between Holyrood (the seat of Scotland's parliament) and the UK government at Westminster (Connolly and Pyper 2020; Cairney 2017). This contentious constitutional context can be a distraction that complicates the work of policymaking matters (Connolly and Pyper, 2020).

In Scotland, as in the rest of the UK, transformation, improvement, and restructuring are common themes associated with efforts to reform public services. Scholars differ on whether the approach to policymaking in Scotland, sometimes known as the 'Scottish Approach', is truly distinctive from the UK policymaking approach or more of an aspirational statement (Housden 2013, Cairney 2020). Although sceptical about the uniqueness of Scotland's reform approaches, Cairney acknowledges the innovation in the policymaking style of the Scottish Government's National Performance Framework (NPF). The NPF, which will be discussed more fully later in this chapter, is an outcome-focused initiative that requires and promotes a a collaborative response.

As with any government-related reform effort, the momentum and drive for reform is complicated by the shifting nature of politics. Joyce (2005, 2021) argues the authority and accountability for policymaking reform is political; thus politicians, with the power and legitimacy granted to them through democratic elections, will make the decisions and take the actions necessary to improve collaboration and rethink leadership in public service agencies. However, political leaders are all subject to five-year political terms, with the associated debates and challenges that each election brings. In addition, inherent boundaries of standard bureaucracy and political decision-making seem ill-fitted to manage the increasing complexity of the public service mission – a complexity that requires a multi-stakeholder response made up of partnerships, networks and collaborations. (Ansell et al 2021; Joyce 2021; Milner and Joyce 2005).

The constitutional context of independence; the politics of political leadership together with the dynamics of accountability and responsibility; and the requirement for multi-actor and multi-structure models of working to address increasingly complex societal problems are all important tensions, conundrums, and considerations that influence and impact the Scottish reform agenda and promotion of collaboration.

Collaboration in Scotland's Public Services

The mid-2000s in Scotland saw an intentional shift towards greater collaboration and partnership among the multiple agencies and organizations that make up the public service sector in Scotland (see Figure 4.1) for services to be designed and built in partnership. The need for partnership and collaboration was one of the core themes to emerge from the Scottish government's Commission on the Future Delivery of Public Services in Scotland in 2011. Partnership and collaboration were also key unifying themes of the National Performance Framework (NPF), an aspirational model for the future of Scottish services. The Scottish government's Scottish Leaders Forum (SLF) would lead the effort to make the recommendations of the Commission and the aspirations of the NPF the reality of how the vast system of Scottish public services would be developed and delivered to the people of Scotland. Below we review in more detail a breakdown of the governmental agencies and initiatives spearheading this effort.

The Christie Commission

The Commission on the Future Delivery of Public Services – commonly known from the name of its chairman, Dr. Campbell Christie, as the Christie Report – published its finding on June 29, 2011(Christie 2011). The Commission's mandate was to better understand the causes of its public service failures or challenges, notably in addressing the needs of the most disadvantaged and vulnerable. For the Christie Commission, nothing less than the radical reform and transformation of public services would be required to improve the quality of services.

The vital role of collaboration and partnership was one of the foundational principles for this proposed reform. 'Our whole system of public services – public, third and private sectors – must become more efficient by reducing duplication and sharing services wherever possible', the report states (Christie 2011, p. vi).

The Commission's findings and recommendations were fully supported by the Scottish National Party-led government, which called not only for public, third, and private sectors to collaborate, but also for greater responsibility and control to be given to citizens and communities (Loeffler et al. 2013). The Community Empowerment (Scotland) Act of 2015

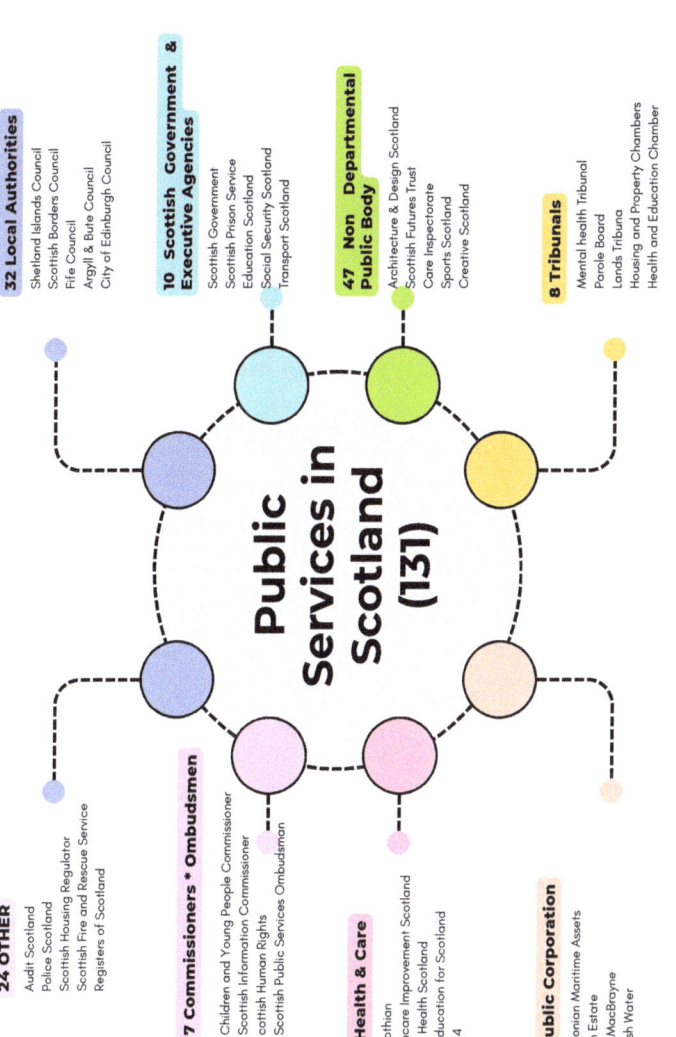

Figure 4.1 Scottish public service agencies and organizations

reinforced this emphasis on expanded community responsibility and control in collaboration with public service providers.

The National Performance Framework

The development in 2011 of the National Performance Framework (Scottish Government 2011, 2018) further emphasized the government's commitment to a collaborative approach to public services. As shown in Figure 4.2, the NPF consists of a series of outcomes and values, expressed in aspirational affirmations, that offer a vision of a future Scotland. Each theme – the environment, human rights, poverty, work, health, and diversity, to name a few of the 11 interrelated themes – has its own statement of broad strategic intentions. 'We tackle poverty by sharing opportunities, power, and wealth more equally,' is one such statement. 'We live in communities that are inclusive, empowered, resilient, and safe,' is another, reflecting again a desired national outcome. These broad strategic intentions offer the agencies, organizations, and businesses of Scotland's public services an organizing structure that supports and enables collaboration (Mackie 2018). For achieving these outcomes requires not just working together across departmental, organizational and sector boundaries but also giving public leaders and managers the space to address how they will achieve these outcomes.

Figure 2 – National Performance Framework (Scotland)

Scottish Leaders Forum (SLF) – The Scottish Leaders Forum (SLF) brings together senior leaders (chief executive level or equivalent) from across public services, third sector organizations, and private organizations that deliver public services. This group, numbering more than 300 at the time of writing, is coordinated and administrated by the Scottish Government. Its goal: building relationships across organizational boundaries – and the thematic boundaries of the NPF – to improve collaborative work. While the Christie Commission and the NPF offered recommendations and aspirational objectives for public service reform, the SLF took the lead to implement and achieve the forward steps and ultimate vision set forth by these two initiatives. The SLF's efforts first took shape through the formation of a workforce development group called 'Workforce Scotland'.

Workforce Scotland – Workforce Scotland was created by the SLF in 2012, gathering several chief executives and senior colleagues from across a wide range of public service organizations. Its mandate was to build on key aspects of the Christie Report. One of the seminal recommendations by the Christie Commission was the need to develop collaborative leadership across the wider public services system. In 2013, Workforce Scotland began developing a national collaborative leadership development programme which would eventually be called Pioneering Collaborative Leadership. Pioneering Collaborative Leadership was based on four components:

- Working with real teams on real work.
- Embedding leadership learning as part of this work.
- Use of Action Inquiry as a method to reflect on the impact on yourself, the group and the wider system, and to determine future action.
- Deployment and development of facilitators to guide the work.

A number of public service teams from across Scotland incorporated The Pioneering Collaborative Leadership programme with the support of two partner consultancies: What Works Scotland (a joint project between the University of Glasgow and the University of Edinburgh) and Research for Real (a consultancy based in Edinburgh led by Dr Cathy Sharp). These partners supported the ongoing learning and evaluation of the programme.

Collective Leadership for Scotland

In 2017, the Pioneering Collaborative Leadership programme and Workforce Scotland were folded into the Collective Leadership for Scotland (CLS) initiative. CLS was led by a small team within the Scottish Government that designed and delivered learning and development activities to better equip public service professionals in their work. The mandate of the CLS team was to build on the learnings from the previous efforts described above, but at the same time approach leadership and collaboration differently. The reason for this shift in approach was concern over the disappointing progress toward achieving the goals set out in the Christie Commission.

CLS programmes were not off-site training courses but rather facilitation support for teams in their places of work, ensuring that the concepts of collaboration, collective leadership, and working within a larger system were directly linked to day-to-day tasks and objectives. In terms of collaboration, CLS programmes focused on the behavioural and relational aspects of working together – how behaviours may need to be adapted and relationships strengthened through openness and trust for collaboration to be effective. CLS places particular emphasis on the complex issues that require collaboration not just within organizations, but across organizational boundaries. CLS worked to help teams to recognize complex issues as systemic issues that require systemic responses and solutions. CLS also focused on helping teams replace traditional top-down leadership with collective leadership capabilities, a difficult but vital new leadership mindset for the new collaborative context of public services.

To achieve its ambitious goals, CLS, as illustrated in Figure 4.3, kept the National Performance Framework at the heart of its approach, but delineated five overarching themes to power the NPF's objectives:

- Growing our ability to work in complex systems.
- Building our capacity for collective leadership.
- Sparking creativity and innovation.
- Working out loud and sharing our story.
- Connecting the system to more of itself.

Figure 3 – Collective Leadership for Scotland Strategy Model
National Performance Framework

The work of the CLS initiative was launched in January 2018 and ran until the project ended in March 2023. The CLS team worked with partners from across Scotland's public services system. The team also reached beyond Scotland, engaging with UK-wide teams to share knowledge and learning. CLS focused on aspects of leadership development in relation to its practice and with its work recognized the importance of working collaboratively and across organizational boundaries and the need for continual learning in order to build the capacity necessary to address systemic issues (*Collective Leadership*, 2018).

Project Lift

As noted above, the collaborative, collective leadership, and systemic mindsets driving the public services initiatives above were sparked and guided by the work of the Christie Commission and the National Performance Framework. In the final section of this chapter, I'd like to mention another major Scottish Government initiative equally inspired and guided by the Christie Commission and the NPF. This initiative, called 'Project Lift', focused on leadership in the Scottish national health care system (NHS Scotland 2019). Formally established in 2018, Project Lift had its genesis in a 2015 NHS leadership and talent management steering group that commissioned research on leadership in the Scottish healthcare system. Project Lift was somewhat different from CLS in that its approach was explicitly built on people and relationships. *Diversity, inclusivity, humility, kindness and compassion*, and *purpose and connections* were all part of what Project Lift called its "ethos" (NHS Scotland 2018).

Building relationships across the health care system, encouraging through an inclusive process the ambitions of aspiring leaders with NHS but also other sectors related to social issues, developing collective and relational leadership within teams, recruiting individuals whose values align with the values of NHS Scotland, and focusing performance appraisals on the values reflected in Project Lift's ethos are key elements this initiative's application of the collaborative, collective leadership, and systemic mindset in Scotland's public services today. Project Lift was replaced by the Leading to Change initiative in October 2022.

CHAPTER 5

The Transformation of Public Services

The previous chapter offered a macro-perspective on public services in Scotland, focusing specifically on collaborative organizations and initiatives. In this chapter, we look at the evolution of public services through the eyes of those working within public services in Scotland at the time of this study. The opinions and experiences of the participants I interviewed offer an insight into their perspective on the practice of public services – that is, how work is done. This perspective includes their experience of working in today's high-expectations environment, the challenges they face, and the reasons they believe alternative collaborative practices are required. Previous chapters have focused on academic theories and government initiatives involving collaboration and collective leadership. This chapters covers the working reality of our topic.

The following participant's comment sets the stage for the chapter by offering an overview of the challenges public service workers face.

The current way of doing things isn't really working. You know, when you work with leaders, whether they are from a council, NHS or any other body, everybody is absolutely trying to do their best. They want to deliver better outcomes for the citizens and communities and deliver their service better.

However, nothing's changing fast enough. We're in this complex system, this world where everything is changing so quickly in terms of technology and expectations. Customer expectations and citizen expectations are absolutely through the roof and the resources and the money available to deliver that is diminishing all the time and the pressure on the system is absolutely incredible and the gap between the people that have and the people that don't have seems to be widening, it's really actually quite scary.

So, to think we can keep doing what we've been doing and just tweak it a little is ridiculous; there is a requirement for something that is really, really different.

That "the current way of doing things isn't really working" was a recurring theme throughout the interviews. Thorough analysis of the interviews (see Chapter 2 for details) revealed eight specific areas of concern relating to how work was done that led to disappointing outcomes or outright failure. Figure 5.1 presents an overview of these eight areas of concern. Although this is not an exhaustive list, the areas of concern listed here were the ones most brought-up by participants when discussing the particular issue of public service practice.

The State of Public Service Practice: 8 Areas of Concern

One of the key insights emerging from public service research is the realization of the **systemic nature** of public services – the need for different organizations and agencies to work seamlessly together as part of a system. However, this seamless collaboration is less evident than in theory given the different cultures, traditions, and ways of doing things among the different agencies. While some agencies might be moving toward greater collaborations, others might still be following the old ways, struggling to cope within the new collaborative paradigm. Instead of being supported by others, staff in many of these organizations find themselves working in isolation – and having to deal with processes that block or complicate rather than facilitate collaboration. Participant P described the counterproductive nature of some of the processes:

.....rather than just talking to one another people were using the process to force one another into a room, which was really counterproductive; a five minute conversation on the phone would have resolved some of the issues that then took ninety minutes in a very expensive meeting

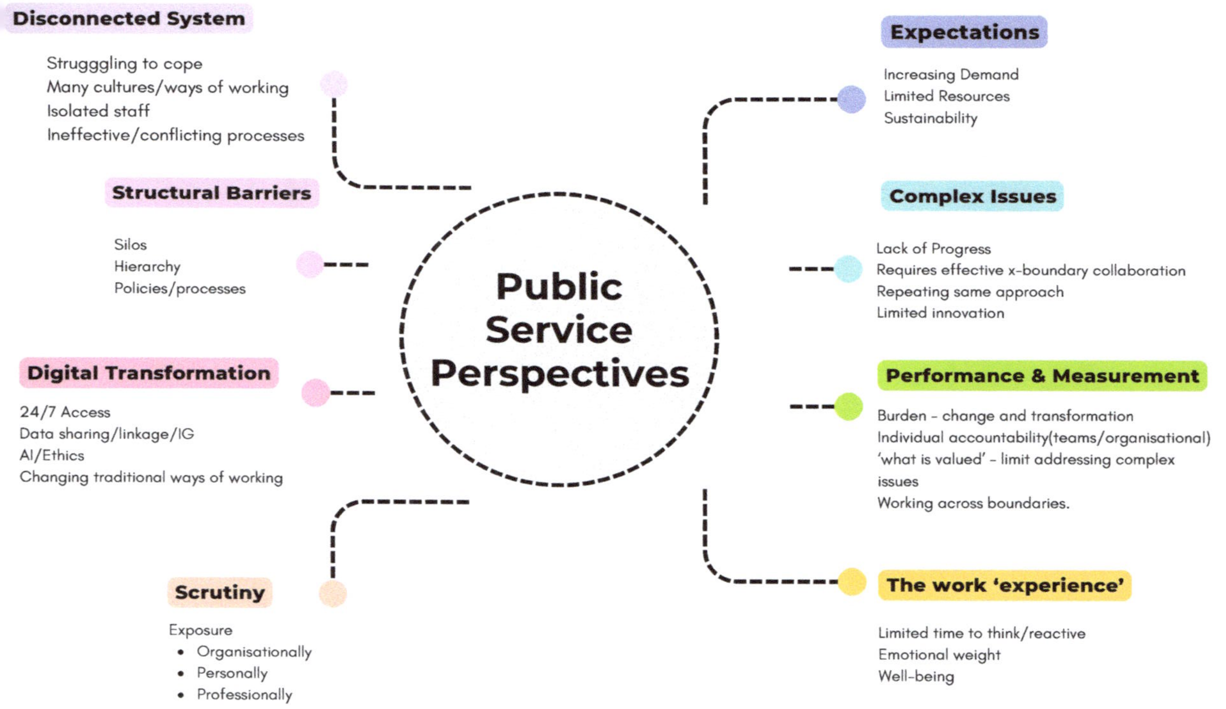

Public Service Perspectives

Expectations
- Increasing Demand
- Limited Resources
- Sustainability

Complex Issues
- Lack of Progress
- Requires effective x-boundary collaboration
- Repeating same approach
- Limited innovation

Performance & Measurement
- Burden – change and transformation
- Individual accountability (teams/organisational)
- 'what is valued' – limit addressing complex issues
- Working across boundaries.

The work 'experience'
- Limited time to think/reactive
- Emotional weight
- Well-being

Disconnected System
- Struggling to cope
- Many cultures/ways of working
- Isolated staff
- Ineffective/conflicting processes

Structural Barriers
- Silos
- Hierarchy
- Policies/processes

Digital Transformation
- 24/7 Access
- Data sharing/linkage/IG
- AI/Ethics
- Changing traditional ways of working

Scrutiny
- Exposure
  - Organisationally
  - Personally
  - Professionally

Figure 5.1 – Contextual perspectives

> *with four, five or six professionals there with a family, making the family uncomfortable, all [of] these softer indicators that people don't always take into account [by] trying to follow the right process.*

In addition to the misalignment of cultures and ways of working among partners in the public service system, a second complication to collaboration cited by the participants was the **structural barriers** they encountered in collaborations. A significant number of organizations and agencies had hierarchical and silo structures: different departments and functions were run as self-contained units each with top-down leadership structures. These types of structural barriers exacerbated attempts to make progress through collaboration. Instead, as described by participants, organizations with different cultures and priorities clashed repeatedly, causing tensions, mistrust and ineffectiveness.

The **digital transformation** of public services has fundamentally changed the way people engage with public services. Customer demands have risen sky high as nothing less than 24/7 access to people and services and immediate resolution is expected. In this new environment, the pressure to respond is acute, and the traditional ways of working and traditional communication strategies and processes are no longer adequate.

One participant gave an example of how the increased access to people had impacted their working environment and experience:

It's a news-driven, fast-paced, social media-influenced environment, where people look to politicians to resolve very complex problems at breakneck speed. That's the environment we live in since the advent of 24/7 news and smart technology: we're in an environment here where someone can tweet the first minister and receive a direct response, which cuts through every sense of hierarchy that previously existed.

The fourth contextual complication raised by the participants involved the high levels of **public scrutiny** they experience today. Public services and their staff have to become increasingly 'transparent' and visible to external examination. Digital developments exacerbate the intrusiveness of this external examination. Leaders, professionals and staff feel increasingly more organizationally and personally exposed – more so than they have ever been before.

Our opening quote spoke about the fifth area of concern related to current public service practice: the growing and shifting **expectations** from customers. Unhelpful processes, misaligned services, and rigid structures, as well as the emerging funding gap in Scotland, added to the pressure on day-to-day working of such expectations. All participants agreed that to better manage demand and improve outcomes, more effective collaboration across boundaries was essential. Participant E lamented the structural barriers that continue to undermine such vital collaboration:

.....traditional forms, traditional structures, traditional funding, they are not cross-cutting. I don't think we're set up in public services to work in that way; we keep saying we want to, but actually everything goes back to either professional silos or funding silos or performance silos and they keep pulling us back.

Complexity is another recurring issue in public services today. For many participants, complex issues challenging those working in public services were not being adequately addressed because of obsolete structures and processes still being used. Traditional technical and planned responses deliver only partial success. Participants were clearly dissatisfied and frustrated at the repeated failure to achieve the desired impact and make things better at a local level.

This frustration is felt in the comments

of Participant O, who argues that additional measures need to be taken into account when considering change and reform beyond structure-led change:

Typically, governments would focus on the restructuring of organizations or changing the funding, performance management regimes, or governance. So public service reform is often spoken about in terms of restructuring things and that has an important role and that can be effective; however, my own view and I think the government's view is that it's not enough on its own.

As we will explore in more detail later, **performance and measurement** brought more frustration than support in collaborative situations. 'What gets measured gets done' is a positive maxim as long as what is being measured needs to get done – something participants did not always feel was the case. Instead, the burden of measurement often undermined the efforts of participants to address complex issues and work across boundaries. Being accountable in multiple directions, external scrutiny, the concern for reputations, and a tricky political landscape were some of the reasons performance measures created pressure for public service professionals.

The work experience:

The day-in-day-out pressure felt by participants from the factors just described hurt their motivation, their well-being, and even the pride in their work – in short, their entire **work experience** became somewhat overwhelming. Focusing, managing new information, and making effective decisions were a strain.

Participant C provided a moving account, within a public service healthcare setting, of the detrimental impact of such an environment on actions and decisions.

When I see people who are busy and under sustained pressure, I see how they lose a sense of their humanity, how they become task-orientated rather than emotionally orientated and often lose the ability to empathize, to connect and to then take meaningful action for the other person.

They may take action, but it may not be with empathy. And I have been in that position, where the pressure of demand, especially in clinical managerial situations, the pressure of the role, or the situation, or a combination of the two, will lead me to be less able to see the uniqueness of the requirements of the individual in front of me. As a result, you revert back to a safety mode, like when a computer crashes and it says, do you want to start in safe mode? You get all the functions, but they are not the same as they are normally. You get people working to a level that is competent and not improper, but they fail to see the bigger picture, they fail to see what's at the edge; so their horizon narrows and their ability to take different points of view is very limited. And judgement becomes more readily given, so you start to see higher levels of blame, looking to other people, less personal accountability.

The Pressures of Collaboration

The Commission on the future delivery of public services (Christie 2011) emphasized the need for collaboration in public services. The participants agreed on collaboration as the best approach to address the challenges facing public services. However, collaboration brings its own set of pressures. Figure 5.2 provides a visual interpretation of 6 key pressure points associated with collaboration as expressed by the participants.

Let's review these six pressure points.

Silos over systems: Conceptually, collaboration is a horizontal phenomenon, with collaborators reaching out and beyond boundaries to collaborators in other parts of the system. Nothing brings collaboration to a halt faster than the existence of silos, which move in a completely different direction. The movement in silos is rigidly vertical: actions and decisions are made or occur vertically, moving up and down a single component in the system segregated from every other component. In an environment of silos, systems change and cross-boundary working becomes nearly impossible – as confirmed by the poor success record experienced by the participants despite their huge efforts made to work towards better outcomes. Such efforts fall short because decisions are made and actions are taken at a service or organizational level without regard to the wider system impact. In some cases, the outcome created an even worse situation either at the core of the change initiative or perhaps somewhere else across the system, which may never even be seen or acknowledged.

Leadership: Another area in which traditional mindsets and approaches conflicted with the needs of collaborative work is found in the area of leadership. As described in Chapter 3, different leadership approaches have dominated in different eras. The most common forms of leadership, however, continue to be the traditional single-individual heroic leader and the more recent transformational leader – both built on the idea

Figure 10 – Collaboration pressure points

of strong leaders leading followers from the front. The participants' experience show heroic and transformational leadership styles clashing with working and leading across boundaries. The reason is that the formal authority from which these leaders draw their power disappears when boundaries are crossed.

Participant F described this conflict well:

If you're in a position of authority, you very quickly forget that you've got formal power; you stop seeing it because people do what you say by-and-large. The leaders start thinking, 'A lot of things will just happen 'cause I am the top dog here,' That is what is hugely challenging when leaders have to work across boundaries and have no formal power and the people in the other organization won't follow what they've said.

Responding to complex issues within collaborations: Participants found that collaborations weakened by structural and leadership issues were in a particularly poor position to deal with complex, often intractable issues. Traditionally, such issues might be addressed with technical, technocratic approaches – approaches that do not work in the context of collaborative, system-wide projects. Worse, once these approaches are programmed and funded, alternative more innovative ideas and possibilities are shut down. Yet, organizations continue to believe that their traditional approaches offered the solutions to these complex issues, refusing to accept the reality of unsuccessful attempts and to talk openly about failure. And any effort dedicated to finding ways to think and work differently on complex issues, or to try out new things are rebuffed as too risky. The frustration among participants was palpable as they struggled to address complex problems that required collaboration within structures and approaches that made collaboration nearly impossible.

Managed collaborations: Participants described collaborations where groups were told to meet, what to discuss, who to invite and who would lead (typically the largest organization or the one with the funds). In these meetings, individuals toed their organizational line. The failure of these types of collaborations are inevitable for they are not in actuality collaborations. The essence of collaboration is dialogue, exchange of ideas, and consensus around actions. When collaborators have no power or freedom, successful collaborations become what some participants called "talking shops" – a combination of polite conversation, power struggles and unsurfaced tensions.

Unsurprisingly, individuals and organizations lose momentum and motivation as months without results or progress pass.

Performance and measurement: We have seen this issue raised earlier in the chapter in the context of the public service practice. Collaboration only heightens the issues in this area. Even in partnerships or collaborations considered to be achieving, participants did not feel that any evaluations of their performance supported and acknowledged their efforts. Participants described how they worked toward a shared goal that spanned organizations, but the infrastructure for setting performance targets, delivering resources, and measuring and rewarding performance outcomes remained encased within the thick walls of individual organizations. Another complication arises with the long-term perspective of collaborations when individuals continue to be judged on short-term outputs and outcomes.

Next level collaboration: All of the participants agreed that collaboration was the key to improved outcomes in public services – which led to some frustration on their part since many collaborations in which they were involved were failing to deliver meaningful change. Participants felt they could and should be achieving more to improve services and outcomes. At the same time, the participants acknowledged the pressures and barriers they faced, delineated in this chapter, that were negatively impacting their collaborative efforts.

In the end, the participants in this study remain committed to the importance of better understanding how individuals and groups can work effectively together to resolve complex issues, make meaningful change, and connect with people across the public service system.

I close this chapter with an optimistic perspective on the continued growth and increasing collaborative intensity of collaborative efforts in public services offered by Participants S:

What I could see over a period of time was a sense of people coming at partnership firstly through mandate, then through a sense that there is purpose in collaborating although still keeping very close to personal and organizational objectives as part of that collaboration. I think what I'm now beginning to see is a real sense that to get to the next level of the implementation of the Christie vision of preventative outcomes and services something different is required.

The remaining chapters of this book present, based on the participant interviews and prior academic research, a new framework that defines the "something different" that is today required to ensure successful collaborative partnerships in public services. This framework is called The Four Principles of Effective Collaboration.

CHAPTER 6

The Four Principles of Collective Leadership

An analysis of the participants' responses and descriptions yielded four distinct but interrelated principles that capture the core components of successful collective leadership. The principles – systems thinking, working emergently, relationality, and inquiry – each reflect four fundamental current ways of thinking and working that need to be adjusted when operating in a collaborative context, as shown in Figure 6.1.

Figure 6.1 The Four Principles of Collective Leadership

The principles are described in more detail in the following sections.

Principle 1. Systems Thinking

Systems thinking refers to the recognition of elements or parts that function as a whole. Everything is connected to everything else, so that working on one part of the system will impact the whole system. For the participants in my study, systems perspective is required for public services due to the wicked and complex issues that public services deal with. Because they are complex, these issues span more than one part of the system.

A Focus on 'the Whole'

Participants agreed that adopting a systems perspective – that is, focusing on the whole and not just a part – required shifting away from the siloed view of the world that dominated in the past. Abandoning silo thinking and planning was considered by participants as the only way to work and lead in a more collective way. Yet, what also emerged from the participants' comments were the problems individuals and organizations had to effect this shift. These problems stem from the barriers and priorities associated with the different parts of the system. For example, the inward-focused way organizations are currently structured and financed impedes a system approach that calls for joint resourcing. Divergent priorities – that is, the draw of individual and organizational priorities over system priorities – is also problematic. To prevent individual and organizational priorities from hampering collaboration, the members of the group must focus on the outcome. As Participant E explained, '...it's a bit about parking the individual agenda and really try[ing] to get into what collectively could we do that would actually shift the outcomes in this area.'

Connections (People and Problems)

A systems approach is not only about recognizing that all parts are connected to each other; it also recognizes that this interdependency requires the types of solutions that emerge when the knowledge and ideas of people from different parts of the system are brought together. For that reason, sharing knowledge, experiences, and stories, as well as learning together, is vital to the development of solutions for wicked and complex problems. As Participant E noted, better understanding of the interdependencies that exist across professions, departments, and

ADOPTING A SYSTEMS MINDSET

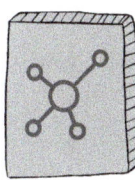

A focus on 'the whole'

Shift from a siloed view of the world towards a systems perspective. Connecting issues and people, transferring knowlede across boundaries and organisations.

Open up Issues

In order to make sense of complex issues and understand the whole we must shift away from traditional notions of problem solving (breaking down and tackling independently).

Diversity

Introduce diverse voices and experiences from across the system, including communities, third and private sector. Alernative views and insights.

Learning together

Taking the time to discuss the nature of the problem, acknowledge the interdependencies that exist across professions, disciplines, departments and organisations.

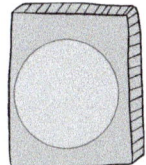

Making connections - people and problems.

Making sense of where potential solutions lie and who with. A gateway into sharing knowledge, experiences and stories, an increased awareness of the invisible threads that bind them.

Figure 6.2 Systems Principle

organizations stimulates new knowledge and learning.

The participants also emphasized the need to explore together the problems faced before rushing towards a plan. As Participant O noted:

We don't at the outset simply say we already know how to do this and here is the project plan and these are the milestones without allowing time for that deeper sense-making process at a collective level, because the minute that you programme[atic] something, you shut down room for that more creative process.

For participants, a systems approach also felt less isolating, as Participant M explained:

There are opportunities to approach a complex issue that you're grappling in within your own area and not making headway to realize that this is [a] system and that you are therefore less alone and isolated with an issue.

Diversity of Voices, People, Experiences

As described above, a systems approach involves an awareness of the interrelationships and connections between the parts of the whole. One of the key strengths of this systems approach in dealing with complexity and uncertainty is the diversity of voices, backgrounds, and experiences represented in the people who are striving to learn together. These people come from across the system, including communities, third and private sector, and can offer to the group alternative views and insights. With not only different ideas and experiences, but also different aspirations, this diverse group is ready to challenge the current ways of thinking and planning.

Holding the diverse groups together and driving them forward in the quest for solutions and reform is a sense that they all share the burden of responsibility associated with solving problems. Participants O explained this well:

I think it's about the shared responsibility. It is about not having the answers and about really seeking to understand the people and the issues that are in the system. It is not assuming that you know what the solution is or what's best for others. It's really believing that everybody's got a contribution to make in figuring that out, quite literally everybody – all of the stakeholders, people that work in the organizations that deliver services, the citizens, the elected members, the board members, and the third sector.

Participant M provided a specific example of how diverse viewpoints reveal the interconnections related to the problems and tasks at hand:

> *For example, if we talk about attainment, you will often get people in education thinking it's an education issue. If we were to widen this out, we can listen to other issues like poverty, employment, housing, all sorts of things that we might want to explore around the issue of attainment.*

The challenge is how to build successful diverse working groups. Participants acknowledge that to invite in and engage with different people at different times required changing the current processes and approaches to working. Such a change was not easy as current practices were based on individual accountabilities and organizational culture and expectations. Joining a diverse group outside of one's silo or organization could increase the strain and pressure felt by workers as they dealt with the personal and organizational risks and pressures attached to shifting to the system perspective. Participant O described this pressure:

> *It's quite different. If you're a civil servant and you're used to going out and speaking at conferences where you're on the podium because you're from the Scottish Government and people look to you as a source of authority or guidance or direction*

... suddenly you're not in that space. Suddenly you're saying I'm here to listen and we don't have the answer to this, this is complex, it is messy, we're going to have to sense where some solutions might lie here ... That's quite a different way of being for a civil servant, let alone a senior civil servant...

Thus, systems thinking opens the door to opportunities and new insights but also to the risk of exposure and vulnerability.

Principle 2. Emergent

An emergent approach is the opposite of a planned approach. One can think of a planned approach to finding a solution or accomplishing a task like driving a car from point A to point B with the directions printed out and laying on the seat beside you. An emergent approach is to get into the car and start driving with a vague notion of point B in your mind, but without exactly knowing where it is or how to get there. As you drive along, you will pick up passengers and in discussions with these passengers and with the help of the passengers' knowledge combined with your knowledge – and trying out different routes and making adjustments as necessary – the route to point B will emerge.

Taking an emergent approach was described by participants as a continuous process of experimentation and adaptation, leading to progress in small to medium incremental steps as new ideas and opportunities emerge. To succeed, the emergent approach needs group members to be open to whatever emerges.

Participant K eloquently described the excitement and uncertainty of working in an emergent way:

It is a big leap of faith, you don't know what you're going to get if you're working in an emergent sort of way. You're kind of rolling towards an outcome, but you don't know definitively. It's iterative, it's expansive, it's mind-boggling.

Participants said working in an emergent way was more useful when grappling with complex, intractable issues than traditional planned approaches. Not having to stay on plan allowed the group to unpack issues that caused problems with day-to-day tasks, which in turn positively impacted long-term goals.

WORKING EMERGENTLY
A LESS LINEAR AND FLUID ROUTE

Different to a planned approach
We are not used to working emergently - instead project plans, agendas and identified roles are the norm. This approach fully embraces change and allows an alternative way of working.

Choosing to work in uncertainty
Conciously electing to work in uncertainty and respecting the process- requires a degree of faith in its ability to present opportunities and to inform action.

Knowing and not knowing
Admitting to not knowing the answer or solution supports a method that provides the opportunity and time to make sense of complexity.

Openness and patience
Working without a plan requires a particular mindset, it can feel uncomfortable, messy, threatening- reverting to familiar methods is a constant pull.

Collective disruption
The whole point of this approach is its disruptive and collective nature, it allows breathing space and oxygen to be brought to a range of people's motivations, beliefs and energies about things that they care about.

Figure 6.3 Emergent Principle

The Emergent Process

For many participants, taking an emergent approach within a collaborative group felt strange and even hard to accept. Participants explained that they were not used to working in that way. The following six points interpreted from the data and supported by participant accounts set out their experience of working in an emergent way.

Knowing and Not Knowing

One of the strengths of emergent working is that it gives permission to take the time necessary to make sense of a complex issue. The group even has permission to declare an answer or solution as out of reach, which provides an opportunity to explore the work together and to develop a deeper sense-making process at a collective level.

Participant E described how acceptance of 'not knowing' allowed the group to move forward:

Coming at this from a point of view of not having to know the answer, and then taking some of the stress off to say well, what is it we need to know, what it is we don't actually know and we're just assuming, sometimes that helps people into conversations.

Choosing to Work in Uncertainty

To work in an emergent way is to deliberately elect to work in uncertainty, which requires faith in the process, as Participant H explained:

You have to really value the process and that this is going to take us somewhere. But you have to be able to work in uncertainty because quite often when people do set aside time, they want there to be a firm action plan, an exact destination that you can reach and want to know exactly what's going to happen. Almost a blueprint of what we're going to do. But I think a key aspect of this work needs to be to be able to work in uncertainty because what you're doing is setting aside time to find out really about the people and about the issues and understand that well to be able to think about the possibilities.

Many participants admitted the challenge of a journey in uncertainty but, as Participant A declared, "it's a journey we have to go on." Participants said they stayed on the journey because they knew that wicked, complex problems required a different approach.

Openness and Patience

Keeping and maintaining an open mind was essential for participants to stay the course. According to Participant O, there must be 'an openness to stay with whatever emerges rather than allow gut reactions to kick in that might say, that's not familiar therefore it's not to be trusted.'

Seeing action differently

Many participants struggled with refraining from taking action, although they knew such action would tip the group into planned mode. Participant A described how a formal leader within the group, 'really wanted to just step in and take control and tell people and he just managed to hold onto a silence, to just allow a contribution, and it absolutely came when he did that.'

Other participants explained that action had to be viewed differently: not as an item to be accomplished and ticked off the list, but rather action in the sense of helping the group move forward with a new attitude or review a new option. Here's how Participant T described a new view of action:

An action is something where you can say tick I've done it, delivered, it's in the plan...

but you can't say, since we last met, I've started to talk differently to my team. But wouldn't it be wonderful to say since we last met several months ago, the team have started taking more interest in the work, they've come up with lots of ideas of how we do things better and it's freeing up my time to do the other things that I need to do.

Collective thinking, Sense-making and Learning

A planned approach is based on meetings and comes with meeting documents, including agendas, minutes, and reports. In the emergent process, especially in the early stages, such meeting accoutrements are distractions. The idea is to sit together and try to make sense of the issue through reflections and stories and questions. The group is not documenting a march forward, but conversing and watching for collective understandings to start to emerge. Not that such an approach is easy, as Participant G observed:

You use different language, it's just a different way of working and thinking and coming at issues and then deciding well what are we going to do. It's hard and the training in how you've always worked is hardwired.

Participant M described the synergistic output that such a discussion generated:

'...being able to work together, something will emerge that is greater than the sum of the people working together.'

Disruption and Discomfort

The emergent process did not elicit a comfortable feeling for many participants. Described as odd, messy, and unfamiliar, it was also, at least to some, creative and liberating. They appreciated that the process allowed, in the words of Participant O, 'breathing space and oxygen to be brought to the range of people's motivations and beliefs and energies about things that they care about.'

This breathing space included silence, certainly a new way to approach a workplace task. Participant C explained the importance of silence:

The silence is as important as the participation and the silence is a part of the participation and you also need to be able to read and understand how others are participating and being present...it's about what is everyone else bringing into this particular mix? How do I understand what's under the surface for all of them? am I open to understanding all of the various truths that might surround a particular issue that are all probably a bit different? and how can I hold all of that to enable the best direction forward, not the only direction forward but the best direction forward?

Participants noted that not everyone was convinced of the power of such different methods. Said Participant J:

'Some people were saying I'm not going back, I don't have time to sit in a room looking at each other.' A colleague of Participant Q had a similar sentiment: 'I'm not going to keep coming to meetings, my time is precious, I'm trying to make a difference.'

Not knowing can be intimidating, and the usefulness of moving forward without a map can be resisted. For those open to the emergent process, however, the unknown is a blank canvas for individual empowerment and collective learning and creativity.

Principle 3. Relationality

Relationality, the need to work in a more relational way, was a recurring theme brought up by many of the participants, who noted that public services are 'full of relationships'. To work in a relational way meant to be aware of their interactions and interconnectedness with others during the work process, especially for work that spanned functional and organizational boundaries and dealt with complex issues. It quickly became clear from the participants' comments that working on the quality of the relationships among group members was as important as working on the task.

Being relational

To be relational entails consciously focusing on relational activities, recognizing, as Participant G explained, that a group of people brought together did not automatically become a team:

Some of the folk had worked together before, one or two knew each other, but most of us were coming together for the first time...so rather than just throwing a whole bunch of people together and saying you are now a football team, and you're expected to go out and deliver, if we're going to be the team, before we get anywhere near a pitch and kick a ball, we need to get to know each other.

Participants noted that being part of the same public service system was not enough to assume that people knew of each other or knew what the others did on a day-to-day basis. It was therefore important to take time as a group to deliberately

BE MORE RELATIONAL
WHAT DOES IT MEAN AND TAKE?

Privilege relationships (above the task)

The quality of our relationships is as important as the task. Pay attention to strengthening them.

We are not a team (yet)

Acknowledge together that we are not yet a team and building strong relationships is not inevitable. Don't jump straight into the task.

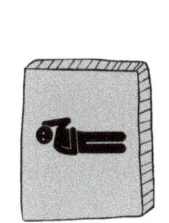

Seek to understand others

Make a concious effort to get to know other peoples work. Go beyond polite conversation, get under the surface.

Agree principles for working

Determine and agree ways of working - sharing ideas, how best to challenge others and be challenged - create our own collaborative culture.

Be open and willing to have your mind changed

Be open to hearing the ideas of others, be curious about how 'you' are being heard.

Figure 6.4 Relationality Principle

focus on relationship development, to learn more about the roles and priorities of others.

Participant J described the outcome of this deliberate relationality:

There was a turning point, and people started to come up with genuine collaborations born from real issues that they were all experiencing, and as we got to know one another's roles, people's preconceived ideas about social work or health started to break down, shadowing started to happen, new learning and new questions started to naturally arise...I shadowed someone where I really thought I knew the service and I didn't at all.

Sharing experiences and stories, especially around failures, was one way collaborators deepened their relationships. Being open to the views and ideas of others and offering to support them also led to higher quality relationships.

Support and Trust

Relationality was essential to building up trust within a group – the foundation of a more nurturing and 'safe' environment where people were more willing to contribute new ideas and take personal risks, which led to more creativity and innovation.

As Participant N said, *'In that kind of environment... people are more likely to come up with suggestions that they might not have done."*

For Participant K, developing such trust was essential when the group members who were engaged in collective work had their own organizational responsibilities and pressures away from the group:

People can come together with a shared vision of what they want to do, to go through a process in which they trust each other enough to be able to put aside agendas to share resources as much as possible, then... go away and do what needs to be done in their own context, and come back together and share the learning from that.

Relational work involved a conscious effort to get to know other people beyond the polite salutations. Participant P described a situation that highlighted the importance of better understanding the work of people in other parts of the system. In this instance, he discovered the unexpected different priorities between social work and education services. Participant P told of meeting a 14-year-old in high school whose mum had gone to Benidorm and left him home alone:

So, I called the local social work manager, I said, you probably know why I'm phoning, I told her who it was, and she said 'right,

I'm really sorry but he's not in my top fifteen today'. That was a wake-up call for me about how different service priorities can be on any given day. How on earth was I to know that there were fourteen other kids in a worse situation that day, but she knew. It's something I shared with my colleagues in my service, because when schools have a priority on their hands, they assume that will be everyone's priority and they can't get their heads round a social worker saying, yes that is a risky situation, but it's not as risky as these other fourteen we're dealing with today, and you're going to have to sit with that risk today.

Meaningful Dialogue

One important lesson offered by participants was the importance of reaching a stage where enough trust is built-up and communication between group members is open enough to enable collaborators to challenge each other. As Participant J succinctly explained: "You're not really collaborating if you're still at the polite stage."

Unfortunately, reaching the stage of an open and constructive dialogue that included the ability to professionally challenge others was not easily achieved. One reason is that challenging others or being challenged oneself is not the normal routine in collaborative work. Participants described being concerned about eliciting a defensive response if they challenged a collaborator.

In addition, attempting to engage in a difficult or tricky conversation can be personally threatening and exhausting. As a result, many people hesitated to raise anything contentious, provocative, controversial or unexpected. Unfortunately, participants were concerned that avoiding conflict or debate led to gaps emerging among services because people preferred to keep quiet rather than risk offending others.

Participant P described the challenge this way:
There was either a general reluctance to do it [challenge each other] or if it did happen it was a bit blunt or a bit hard to take. One of the aspects that's been really positive about it is people just acknowledging that we're in a relationships business and we really need to focus in on the quality of professional working relationships in order to get to the safer place where we can constructively challenge one another a bit more.

To create this safer place, several participants explained that they worked together to create 'a set of principles' to guide their collaborative practice. Creating this set of principles gave group members the opportunity to collectively acknowledged that they would inevitably disagree, and that constructive disagreement was to be encouraged rather than discouraged. Without this permission for constructive disagreement, collaborators may hesitate to share difficult information or observations or creative new ideas or solutions to intractable issues. This, in turn, could lead to issues with the delivery of quality services and care, and inefficiencies within collaborative groups.

In addition, many noted this shift from politeness within groups towards a more healthy form of dialogue mitigated the experience of feeling isolated. Participant J described the freedom of open dialogue:

Before I went into this, I might have felt a bit worried about somebody telling me the way I was doing my job was a bit clunky. Now it feels okay, it was very empowering and reassuring to feel okay about somebody saying, actually you could do that better or differently or that's not working for us the way you're doing that. Taking feedback feels okay now.

In the best collaborations, group members are not only able to accept the 'gift' of constructive feedback, they are also open and curious about the ideas of others. And they are willing to have their minds changed.

Principle 4. Inquiry

All of the participants agreed on the importance of inquiry in a collective leadership approach. An inquiry mindset is a mindset that places exploration and discovery at the heart of how members of a group work together and achieve outcomes. Inquiry is accomplished through curiosity, questioning, listening, suspending judgement, and reflection. Areas of inquiry include how we work together in groups, how to understand the roots of and resolve complex issues, and the impact of our own values, behaviours, and beliefs.

Participant M described the shift required to adopt the practice of inquiry:

Inquiring and being able to listen to each other at depth is part of collective leadership, not turn taking, but being able to really listen, and to understand diverse perspectives, and from that hear different views to test out different actions. Inquiry takes place at the personal and group level, to evaluate or to reflect on what impact does that have on the wider system and then to recognize, what other questions does that lead us to, and to share the learning.

Group Process

How groups work together was one of the most salient areas of inquiry raised by the participants in the context of collaboration and collective leadership. This line of inquiry was based on questions such as 'how can we do our work, with these people, in this environment?' and 'what helps us and what gets in the way?'

In sparking answers to these questions, the inquiry approach guides groups toward a conversation built around sharing expectations and values and learning from each other.

Complex Issues

Approaching complex issues with an inquiry mindset is a significant departure from traditional approaches that favour jumping to a solution or creating a 'to do' list. One major difference is the intentional decision to take the time one needs to investigate all aspects of the problem. Using this time to ask the obvious and not so obvious questions will surface insights and a better understanding of the issue, which would have been missed without the inquiry approach. In some cases, for example, careful inquiry revealed that the assumed main problem was in fact not the main problem. The inquiry approach,

TAKING AN INQUIRY APPROACH

The group process

A collective inquiry into how groups work together can help provide useful insights - how can we do our work, with these people, in this environment? and what helps us and what gets in the way?

Hold a different kind of conversation
Venturing into sharing expectations and values, encourages a learning culture tuned into what make a group work well and why.

Careful questioning
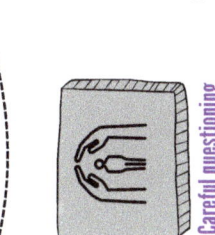
Starts with listening, ask questions to clarify, probe, extend, help others refine their responses 'tell me more about this...' 'give people the space to go into more depth.

Self-awareness

Being really aware of our own behaviour and the impact we have on others. Letting go of ego, advocacy and reflecting on deeply held assumptions and perceptions.

Quest for fresh learning

This can be achieved through the sum of 'programmed instruction' (what has long existed, been told and accepted) and 'questioning insight' (drawn from learning something new about the issue, self and others).

Figure 6.5 Inquiry Principle

according to the participants, also focuses efforts on constructive listening and understanding rather than counter-productive finger-pointing.

Participants referred to the importance of drilling deeply into the issues, enabling all collaborators to fully understand all the facets of the problem. At the same time, questioning and listening also helped the group 'map out' the bigger picture. With this comprehensive exploration of the issue, the group, motivated and committed, could decide on the collective action to take.

Two words often used by participants help explain the power of inquiry were 'noticing' and being 'curious'. With the following anecdote, Participant J illustrates why these words are important:

> *I asked one of the families – because I know that vulnerable families can sometimes bounce from one service to another, we sometimes don't get to the root of the issue – how are you feeling about this ending? The mum became really emotional; the family worker was very shocked at this. She said, 'I had no idea she was worried about ending.' I said that when it ends, families come back to us and say that its ended too soon, or not ended in the right way; she said, 'Right, I'm going to change*

the whole way I do endings as I'd never really thought about that.

Self-awareness

Turning outward and listening to others is a vital element of inquiry, but so, according to the participants, is turning inwards: inquiring into the self, seeking unfiltered self-awareness was a valuable practice for anyone engaged in collaborative work.

As Participant R explained:

It's that sense of being really aware of your own behaviour and the impact of your behaviour on others and seeing yourself as part of the system that everybody has a valid place within and something to contribute.

Participants believed that becoming more aware of one's own individual thought and behaviour patterns can help build empathy and in turn better understand others. Individuals with an inquiry mindset are willing to suspend judgement and are open to having their minds changed.

They are also not afraid of letting go of their ego and the need to convince others. Instead, they strive to consider how others see them and are willing to internally interrogate themselves – all of which helps to support collective work.

Digging deep into themselves, individuals with an inquiry mindset will reflect on their deeply held assumptions and perceptions. They will also explore their individual world views as well as those of others.

This level of self-inquiry, according to the participants, is more than an intellectual exercise, because the intellect does not give us all the answers about ourselves. Those engaged in self-inquiry, therefore, must look to other sources of knowledge, notably the emotional elements of ourselves, such as our feelings, beliefs, and attitudes. Participant M referred to this as 'a physical way of knowing rather than intellectualizing.'

I close this discussion of the four principles with a quote from Participant I, who eloquently describes the power of listening as part of collaborative practice:

I think we still see people having a real 'ah-ha' moment having been listened to for three minutes; my goodness what are we doing if people have never had that experience before?

In this chapter, we broke down the collaborative practice of collective leadership into four principles. In the next two chapters, we continue to explore the learnings from the participants, notably, in Chapter 7, related to how collective leadership is different from traditional approaches, and in Chapter 8, the benefits of collective leadership.

CHAPTER 7

How Collective Leadership Is Different

In the previous chapter, we looked in detail at the process of collective leadership, which is built around the four principles of systems, emergent, relational, and inquiry. In this chapter, we show how the application of collective leadership based on the four principles is different from a traditional collaborative approach. The four principles in this chapter are not treated as distinct elements as in Chapter 6, but instead analyzed and explained as one collective leadership process.

To successfully apply collective leadership, the collaborators must first be prepared to have *a different view of leadership*. They must abandon the traditional idea of "heroic" leadership – the individual 'hero' who will take the lead, guiding his or her followers down the path to success. Heroic leaders acquire their authority and power through their formal position in the hierarchy, often designated by a powerful title which demands deference and obedience from the followers. Heroic leaders often have a mindset that they are in the best position to find the solutions – or lead the organization in finding the solutions – to the problems that need to be addressed and resolved.

The application of collective leadership begins with the recognition that in the face of the complex, 'wicked' problems with which public services are dealing with today, no single individual can be the hero of the organization. As Participant B explained:

If we think about the complexity of the context and the sorts of issues that we're facing across those services, they cannot be, if they ever could be, solved by a top-down leadership or a small number of people in formal leadership roles.

Relinquishing the concept of the heroic leader is not so easy. Participant F said it well:

Letting go of the notion of a quick fix and that you're going to be the heroic leader, it's so ingrained in all of us. [Collective leadership] requires you to actually temporarily take off your corporate armour, your emblems of corporate legitimacy and authority, your title and your role and your formal authority.

An Alternative Perspective on Leadership

Letting go of the hero concept is only the beginning. Collective leadership requires accepting an alternative perspective of leadership in which leadership is a dispersed function, because the sources of knowledge and authority that gives individuals the ability to lead are not acquired through position or titles or leadership development but through their lived experience, values, and motivations. The challenge, given that followership is not required or demanded, is to convince others of the path you are putting forward. 'Everyone's got levels of influence,' said Participant A, and explained how:

They can communicate with neighbours, colleagues, partners. How you do that, what do you take out of the room and what are you going to share, what are you going to try and rally people into contributing to, how are you going to make links to what it is we're trying to do here into what goes on in your day-to-day life and about bringing others into it – that's the leadership bit: talking to others, persuading others, sharing with others, encouraging others.

Power and Empowerment

One of the greatest challenges to implementing a collective leadership approach is disentangling the issues it raises related to power – who has it, how is it distributed, how to deal with leaders used to power within their organizations, and so forth. Collective leadership challenges power norms and behaviours that have become entrenched over the years. For this reason, it is difficult for individuals in traditional leadership roles to give up leadership responsibilities – and for those not in traditional leadership positions to accept these responsibilities.

Understandably letting go of power is difficult for those in traditional, hierarchical leadership roles, who may be so used to power that they don't fully realize the power they have... until they lose it. As Participant F explained:

If you're in a position of authority, you very quickly forget that you've got formal power... [which] is hugely challenging when leaders have to work across boundaries and have not got formal power and the people in the other organization won't follow what they've said.

Even in cross-organizational collaborative groups, some leaders still don't realize that they are no longer in a position of power. Participant A described how this happens:

If you've got really powerful senior people from one of the key organizations [in a collaborative group] they've got so much power over the rest of the group that they don't even realize it and the rest of the group don't always realize the power they've got but they do defer to them a lot.

Addressing these challenging power dynamics requires unequivocal trust and support among the group's members. Such support and trust are achieved when all group members feel they have a voice – when their opinions and experiences, no matter what their official role or position in their organizations, will be listened to and considered by all. And it requires *formal* permission from senior leaders to let others take leadership roles

Privileging Relationships Above Tasks

As noted above, collective leadership cannot work without trust. For this reason, building strong, deep relationships is an urgent need rather than a 'nice-to-have' feature of traditional hierarchical leadership. Getting to know each other and sharing insights and stories sets the foundation for being able to then collectively address and agree on the solutions and next steps for the tasks at hand. Participant O described the emphasis on relationship before task:

Change is more successful when you also address the more relational aspects of this, and those relational aspects are by definition collective. Because the central inquiry shifts from being 'what do I already believe to be the answer or what can you persuade me of which would be a better solution' to 'what does life feel like to be you in your role right now, what matters to you and where do you sense future possibilities; can we both together engage in a place where we have temporarily suspended our pre-existing assumptions and beliefs and discuss future possibilities.

Anchoring Change in a Redefined Culture

For many participants, collective leadership was especially applicable for small scale 'local' issues, issues that were directly in front of them – that affected their day-to-day concerns, for example – as opposed to more long-term, wider scope transformational issues and initiatives. Transformational change is not impossible but requires a more complex and prolonged process. Collective leadership, therefore, was effective for more grounded change, i.e., change that involved specific actions leading to specific outcomes related to, for example, processes, service redesign, or policy revisions. This kind of change sets more feasible goals for collective leadership, as explained by Participant A.

What collective leadership supports is very small initiatives or very small projects that may grow into transformation, but they may not. If you think you're trying to achieve transformation it makes the stakes very high. So, it is about transformation but it's not just about transformation. Sometimes it's a tiny different corner in the area you're working in and that won't feel like transformation when you're working on it but that doesn't mean it won't lead to it.

Working with the Gaps

Collaboration, especially across organizational boundaries, will inevitably reveal gaps or zones of blurriness, such as: differences in knowledge and processes among organizations; lack of a common language; different and often competing organizational structures or cultures; and different, deeply held assumptions and perceptions – the latter relating not only to organizations within the public service system, but to users and citizens as well. These are serious gaps that need to be bridged, and the data in the research shows that collective leadership plays an important role in building these bridges.

The shared sense of empowerment and responsibility that comes with collective leadership – the sense that we all have our part to play – spurs people to fill the gaps. Yes, there may be differences in levels of knowledge, cultures, or language, but these differences can be overcome in a trusting, outward-looking environment – an environment where experiences and reflections are shared across the gaps. Participant P described the environment that enables a collective form of leadership to work:

If you do trust and respect and have a level of understanding that we all do difficult, important jobs, it doesn't mean that you're more important than me, and it doesn't mean you can tell me what to do, as our relationship is secure enough for us to have difficult conversations without falling out.

Understanding Complex Causality of Problems

The complexity of the issues faced by public services makes it less possible for one individual to have all the answers. Having more individuals (and hence more perspectives and experiences) involved in the decision is one reason for the effectiveness of collective leadership. However, collective leadership works not just because of increased numbers but because of a different process or approach to decisions. In fact, one might say the approach is less on 'making a decision' and more on 'resolving a problem,' which entails getting to the root cause of the problem. For behind these problems are often a tangled web of causes and origins linking to other elements. Participant G put it well:

This is a complex system with a whole

> *variety of interconnections...You jump in at one place and it very quickly takes you off in another direction.*

Untangling these webs and uncovering eventual solutions takes time and careful thought, but also creative approaches and new ideas. And it takes the trust and openness that is characteristic of collective leadership. Participant A gave us a concrete example of how this works:

> *The police and the fire brigade weren't quite sure how this would link to us at the moment but they were quite thoughtful and listening. Then they would say 'actually we're doing an event' or 'we've got some officers doing some work in that community' and it was about making really small links in some cases.*

Support and Facilitation

Collective leadership represents a fundamentally different way of working, of interacting with others in your hierarchy and others from outside organizations, and of taking and sharing responsibilities. Implementing such change in the traditional ways and patterns of working does not come easy; developing the relationships, the unique processes, and the new attitudes involved requires support and skilled

How Collective Leadership Is Different

facilitation. The Collective Leadership for Scotland (CLS) team was instrumental in providing such support and facilitating the change. Participant G described the importance of such support.

I think if we hadn't had the input from [the facilitator] we probably would have gone about it in a similar way as we do other things...now we have moved in the direction, we don't call it an agenda, we call it a session plan, we don't call it minutes, we call it our learning notes, and we've kept with that even when [the facilitator] stopped working with us.

Participant F offered a view on the process from the perspective of a facilitator:

Looking at the facilitation process, one of the things I'd be looking for would be the group's ability to work constructively with differences of opinion, so getting on well. You can interpret that in different ways. A cozy group I would feel was not doing very well, a group that was making me feel quite uncomfortable, although I might not like it, if they were obviously not splintering into pieces but persevering through difficult sessions would seem to me an indicator of doing something worthwhile.

The Importance of Learning

Collective leadership is a learning experience – learning together and from the facilitators on how to work differently, but also learning from the knowledge and experiences of others. Being open to learning is essential for collective leadership to successfully lead to reaching a consensus and taking action on the path forward. As Participant M explained:

The greatest depth of learning takes place by learning through real work with the team you're working with in real time on the issue that you're working with.

Participant A described how facilitators led this learning:

When we were talking about it in meetings and we were asking, 'What's going on for you?' 'What questions are you holding?' 'What's happened since the last time?'... we were really capturing the quotes that people were using so that we could use them again. Then when I was having off-line conversations with x, [I would say] remember when so and so said this? That was really powerful. So, it's about making sure we didn't lose any of that and feeding it back in later.

Communicating this Work

One of the challenges of collective leadership is a lack of clarity – at least the clarity found in traditional leadership structures and processes. With collective leadership, there is no clear-cut hierarchical structure, no clear-cut delineation of responsibilities, no clear-cut organizational boundaries, and an emphasis on learning and exploration as opposed to deadlines. As noted above, facilitation support and an openness to learning help those involved with collective leadership to see past the blurriness to the method and rationale of this approach. Communicating how and why the process works to those outside the process is a major challenge, given the blurred parameters described above. Participant N eloquently described why this communication is so difficult:

[Collective leadership] is a much more multi-disciplinary, multi-theory, multi- leadership style, more a banner. People find that really difficult as we're so used to there being a model that you follow whereas actually the level of complexity in which we're working, one model, one approach, will almost never fit more than one context.

Measuring and Evaluation

Measuring and evaluating the success of the kind of public service efforts to which collective leadership is applied – that is, complex wicked issues crossing organizational boundaries and not easily isolated – can be challenging. In addition, the outcome goals of collective leadership are wider than typical goals since collective leadership aims to understand the root causes of issues before attempting any solutions or changes. Measurement can in fact be counterproductive if it constrains or hurries the process. Participant S clearly illustrated the problem:

The temptation is just to say no, the problem is x and to put a measurement framework around x, but maybe the problem is x in combination with y and make sure in tackling y that you don't do any harm to z and that kind of framework is not intuitive to us.

Capacity and Skills

For collective leadership to be successful, the individuals involved must have the capacity for collaboration – in other words, the skills and the resources to effectively work with others. An important element or prerequisite for developing this capacity is a strong belief in the benefits of collaboration in dealing with complex issues. Participant G noted that frustration with past efforts can lead to this belief, or at least to the will to try something different.

We've been at some of these issues for years/decades, so the idea is let's try something different because we know that previous solutions haven't made the impact that we would want. A lot of people, particularly from agencies, are brought up in an environment and training that directs you towards, identify the problem, identify your options, implement the solutions. The issues we're charged with trying to address through the partnerships are much more difficult than that and you have to pull yourself back from the normal desire to jump in and take action.

These are some of the key implications and considerations related to the implementation of collective leadership. In the next chapter, we review individual and group learnings that emerged from collective leadership collaborations.

CHAPTER 8

The Benefits of Collective Leadership

As highlighted in the previous chapter, collaboration with collective leadership is an ongoing learning experience. In this chapter, we look a bit more closely at the opportunities presented by collective leadership for members of a group to develop individually and grow as a collective.

Opening Out

In 2006, Peter Senge published his seminal book, *The Fifth Discipline*, in which he argued against the prevailing notion that to resolve complex problems required breaking them down into smaller pieces and addressing these smaller pieces individually. Senge proposed, on the contrary, that complex issues and challenges needed to be approached from a systems perspective, which is one of the four principles of this book. Instead of isolating and breaking down problems, collective leadership calls for 'opening up' or 'opening out' problems – that is, understanding how they fit with other parts of the system and how this connection to systemic elements informs the search for solutions.

In line with the work of Senge and other scholars who observed wicked and complex issues from a systems perspective, participants often remarked on the complexity of the problems faced by public services, and the need to take a systems approach to find solutions. Only then would their efforts lead to substantial change and improvement.

Fostering Diversity

The opening-out mindset of collective leadership described above fosters greater diversity, bringing in different and alternative perspectives, knowledge, and experiences from across the public service system – including colleagues, communities, citizens, the third sector, and the private sector. A broad group of partners drawing on this diversity leads to new ideas and innovation that would be less likely with traditional top-down leadership and traditional inside-out approach.

The diversity of group members impacts not only the input of the process – in terms of experience and knowledge, for example – but also outcomes in terms of needs and priority concerns. That is, traditionally a leader may pre-determine an agenda that then guides the group's efforts; through collective leadership, the group may be more sensitive to what is 'local' and of value to stakeholders, including end users and citizens. Participants in my study described how input from others was actively sought with the goal of including knowledge and learning from alternative views – or as one participant described it, 'getting the system in the room'.

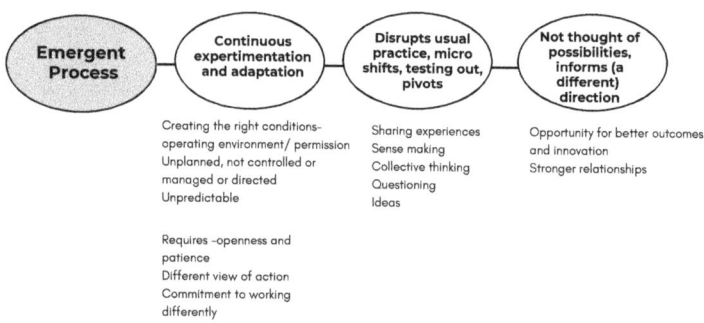

Figure 8.1 – Understanding the emergent process

Disrupting Usual Practice

'Plan the work and work the plan' may be a familiar refrain, but it is the opposite of the emergent approach, another of the four principles of collective leadership. Addressing complex systemic issues requires disrupting the usual practice and allowing solutions and outcomes to emerge from the diversity and open thinking of collective leadership. Figure 8.1 illustrates how an *emergent process* – a process that is deliberately unplanned and unpredictable – sparks a different kind of conversation, manifested through collective thinking and sense-making and shared experiences, which then leads to improvement opportunities and innovation.

Change and Transformation

As opposed to a top-down, direct-planned approach, an emergent process can chart a path to eventual transformation in a different way. The emergent process encourages continuous experimentation and adaptation, which leads to small-to-medium incremental change, but it is these micro changes that lay the foundation for transformational change down the line. This path was evident in my data. Participant L, for example, described the efforts of a collaborating group to improve processes and procedures; the group agreed to create one referral from the twelve different versions then in existence, an indication of potential transformation to come.

The unplanned emergent process with its emphasis on experimentation and exploration does not only offer a path to the resolution of problems but also a way to the functioning of the collaborative group. Because these groups are made up of many stakeholders representing a number of organizations, focusing on how they can function better – that is, how group members can work more effectively together – is key to their success. As a number of participants pointed out, the emergent process can be 'messy' and this messiness and lack of clarity in what lies ahead can lead to tensions within the group. As a result, the temptation to return to the stability and comfort of a planned process is never far away and must be resisted with the important help of leaders giving the group permission to move forward without a plan, and facilitators who can help guide the group in this effort.

Not Knowing

A key finding from my study concerns collaborating members recognizing the complexity of the problems they are dealing with. When they fully understood this complexity, they were more willing to trust an unplanned, collaborative approach to resolving these problems rather than put their faith in a typical, technical planned approach. In addition, 'not knowing' together what exactly lay ahead bound the group members more closely; it also freed them to be more creative and take risks. This freedom stemmed from the fact that that no-one was obliged or expected to lead, manage, or direct them; no-one was expected to step forward with the plan. The plan was open to their making. One can see how the emergent approach is an approach of opportunity

The Benefits of Collective Leadership

– the opportunity to work on complex problems as a group and integrate collective thinking; the opportunity to try different working styles; the opportunity to create a shared understanding – all of which leads to an alternative view of action.

Shared Meanings

A collaborative group encompasses a wide range of individuals, each holding their own beliefs, opinions, and values, and each representing a mix of organizations, departments, and professions with differing goals, missions and priorities. It takes an intense focus on relationship-building to weave all these different practices, priorities, perceptions, and attitudes into the fabric of a group so they can then be used to develop shared meanings and understandings. Creating the proper conditions that will break down these barriers, preconceptions, and assumptions is the work of the group, even before the task or purpose that brought the group together in the first place.

One approach is to develop micro-cultures within collaborative groups, within which all members agree upon parameters of positive behaviours and open but respectful communication – thus constructing, if you will, a 'safe container' for the group to interact and learn (Senge et al. 2015; Raelin 2017).

The participants noted that the importance of differentiating between the cultivation of personal relationships, centered on the needs of the individuals, and the development of quality relationships for collaboration. It is not enough to be nice, polite and friendly, or to flee conflict or confrontation, which are characteristics of personal relationship-building. Quality relationships for collaboration require, according to the participants, honest feedback, and the courage to risk conflict for the greater good. The participants in my study were often frustrated with 'polite' yet unproductive collaborations, as group members suppressed or moderated their contribution at the expense of the group goal.

Emotional Cognizance

Relationships are built on human connection, and human connection often involves the expression of emotions. Group members are encouraged to offer in 'every day' discussions personal reflections about past collaborative failures or projects, for example as a tool to begin and sustain conversations. Participants welcomed the chance to introduce feelings about their work as they were developing relationships with others. This emotional openness sparked meaningful dialogue, strengthening the relationships and improving the collaborative work. Emotions are often considered manifestations of an individual state when in fact, as many scholars note, they are relational (Lopez-Kidwell et al. 2018; de Rivera and Grinkis 1986). Participants in this study agreed with the supportive role of emotions and felt free to be emotionally conscious of not only how *they* felt within the collaboration, but also, and importantly, how others might feel. They were also ready to engage emotionally with the task – a far cry from rational, planned approaches where 'emotions' are considered an unwelcome addition to decision making (Dickinson and Sullivan 2013).

Trust and Power

My study clearly pinpoints the development and preservation of trust as a key characteristic required for successful collaboration. One of the greatest threats to trust among collaborators is the consolidation and/or misuse of power – a threat whose presence is felt even more strongly in the context of collective leadership. The tendency of larger organizations wielding control over others, for example, looms large.

For many participants, the threat of power imbalances was realized; they watched with increasing frustration as collaborations were controlled and 'managed.' The collective leadership process supports the effort to mitigate and confront power issues. First, by definition, collective leadership rejects the appointment of a single leader or organization to direct the group or make decisions. Second, working through the tensions of collaborating without a leader is itself an important step in building trust. Agreeing on how power will be shared is a major element in agreeing on how the group would work together, which leads to trust (Torbert 2004).

Some scholars argue that achieving small wins on the tasks helps resolve power issues, with the small wins strengthening the trust among the group and illuminating productive power relationships (Vangen and Huxham, 2003). My study, in contrast, takes a different approach, recognizing the importance and value of moving forward on the task, but arguing that the group should focus on building trust before reaching any decision or consensus on task-related actions.

Practicing Leadership

As collective leadership turns the tables on the assumptions, processes, and relationships of traditional leadership, practicing collective leadership requires different skills and attitudes.

In Table 8.2 below, I have laid out the five themes that encapsulate the meaning behind the leadership activities in a collaboration. They are: communication, empathy, courage, empowerment/agency and relationship building.

My findings have some similarities with 'the leadership-as-practice development model' prepared by Salicru (2020), whose 5Cs model included the 4Cs of Raelin (2003) – concurrent, collaborative, collective, compassionate – and added a fifth C: co-creative. My table below aligns with the sentiment, principles and descriptions provided by both scholars. For example, Raelin talks about how offering one idea can stimulate a whole new set of actions and Salicru suggests that leadership can take place by more than one person at the same time. In my study, participants described situations where an individual chose to remain silent in order to allow others to contribute. Participants also described instances where one idea was mooted, which changed the entire nature of the conversation and the actions that followed.

Practising Leadership				
Commu-nication	Sharing learning and stories of experience, successes and failures	Making connections with others	Distilling information, translating across boundaries	Freeding back to individual organisation and colleagues, being transparent about the process
Courage	Challenging others and being challenged	Creativity	Taking personal and collective risks	Contributing ideas
Rela-tionship building	Developing trust	Active and deep listening	Silence	Curiosity/interest
Empathy	Consideration of multiple agles of thinking	Representing others	Helping others to understanding the process	
Empow-erment/agency	Taking power and giving power	Making decisions and taking action		

Table 8.2. Practicing Leadership

Self

An inquiry-led approach is an approach, as the name implies, based on learning through asking questions and being questioned. This questioning is driven by the desire to uncover different perspectives, to challenge both oneself and others. (Ringer 2007; Raelin 2019). Emotions are also permitted in the inquiry approach. Note the inquiry does not mean inquisition; this approach is about discovery not prosecution. The goal is to use this approach to work together and find a consensus on the path forward. For this reason, inquiry must be conducted in a sensitive, listening way. Conflict is turned into understanding and then understanding into action (Vangen and Huxham 2003; Raelin 2017).

Morris (1991) refers to this approach as 'questioning insight' (drawn from learning something new about the self and others). If a conflict or tension exists between two people, for example, instead of countering each other, this approach calls for trying to understand why the other person is so steadfast in their opinion. Working through tension in this positive, productive, and open way leads to better relationships and a better understanding of the issue at hand. In this way, addressing the task begins by addressing the tension among collaborators.

The questioning insight approach stands in contrast to what Morris calls 'programmed instruction', which is based on what has long existed, been told and accepted. Morris notes that one does not negate the other; questioning insight and programmed instruction can be combined, thus offering a more complete learning package on which to build collaborative work – an attitude reflected in the responses of the participants in my study.

As one of the four principles to emerge from this study, the inquiry approach was valued by the participants as a way to improve practice and outcomes. Inquiry is a way to use the lived experiences of collaborators to inform the decisions and actions of the group, which resonated with the participants; after all, they identified as being part of the public service system and therefore stakeholders in the very problems their groups were addressing.

Mutuality

The inquiry process, which does not shy away from conflict, strengthens relationships because it is based on mutual respect for the other – a mutual understanding and appreciation of the other's shared commitment to and passion for the work. It also reflects what Schein (2013) calls 'here and now humility': I ask you questions because you may know something I don't know. Such humility and mutual respect are especially important, according to the participants, because of the complexity of the problems being addressed: these problems require a range of inputs based on alternative experiences, processes, and understandings. The self is not enough.

Thomson and Perry (2006) describe the concept of 'complementarity' in collaboration, in which members of a group give up the right to pursue their own individual or organizational interests at the expense of others. In the collective leadership process, however, no group members are giving up anything for the other because everyone is pursuing a shared outcome that they collectively wished to achieve.

CHAPTER 9

The Time Is Now

Collaborative work led by collective leadership represents a significant departure from the current approaches and attitudes to work and leadership in the delivery of public services. This chapter explores why there may be an appetite for moving away from the current collaborative and leadership practices. Based on the responses from the participants in my study, the motivation for incorporating the new approaches described in this book stem from five sources:

New perspectives on leadership. Participants were prepared to explore new approaches to leadership that challenged traditional leadership assumptions and practices.

Dissatisfaction and frustration with past collaborative experiences. Many collaborations often failed to achieve the desired outcomes, and even successful results could be undone by misunderstandings and conflicts.

Dissatisfaction with the effectiveness of the centrist public service model. Structural boundaries and an emphasis on rational and technical solutions undermined collaborative work.

The challenge of wicked issues. The old ways are believed to inadequately prepare public services to deal with complex issues that cross organizational and functional boundaries.

Restrictive performance measures.

Performance measures based on individual and organizational responsibilities fail to encourage and support work at the multi-stakeholder collaborative level.

All of these issues present challenges but possibilities for improvement for public service leaders, as I explore in more detail below.

Shifting Perspectives of Leadership

The participants indicated their scepticism of the concept of the heroic individual who, alone, has the authority and superior knowledge necessary to guide the others. They placed their trust, instead, in leadership that emerged from practice and process (Carroll et al. 2008). Traditional leadership was not summarily dismissed; it was simply felt that a collective leadership style would be more effective to address current, complex public service issues.

Shifting from traditional to collective leadership is not simply a redistribution of authority from the individual to the collective. Such a redistribution is the outcome of a process approach to leadership – that is, the collective leadership of the group emerges as group members interact and collaborate on shared concerns and develop a consensus on the path forward. It was this idea of leadership emerging from the process – rather than leadership being assigned, based on hierarchy, to lead a process – that the participants were willing to consider. Participation in leadership was also expanded to include citizens and communities.

Frustrated Collaborations

Many participants were attracted to the concept of collective leadership because of frustrating experiences with previous collaborations that ended in failure. Often, these previous collaborations were undermined by group members holding on to their organizational mandates, instead of fully committing to cross-organizational collaboration. As a result, the dialogue and exchange of ideas among the group was not as open and free as it needed to be, leading to underwhelming actions and outcomes. The preference for polite conversation over in-depth interactions that tackled the tough issues did not help. And even if any progress was made, this progress would unravel because of confusion or a lack of commitment.

Change is never easy. Deeply ingrained working practices and assumptions are not easy to dislodge, and less so when conflicting priorities – short-term over long-term, organization over cross-organizational collaboration – pull people back to the old ways. As much as participants believe in the collective leadership process, they also believe that building greater collaborative capacity was essential if the process was to be successful.

Figure 9.1 The Challenge of Collaboration

Figure 9.1 summarizes the seven core challenges that hamper collaborations. These seven challenges are: inflexible structures and silos, power imbalances, leadership tensions, planned instead of emergent approaches, evaluation and measurement, conflicting interests and motivations, and technology data and security – the latter dragging down the exchange of information and knowledge.

Restrictive Public Service Model

Collaboration across organizations is inherently difficult. Collaboration is even more difficult when hierarchy, bureaucracy, rigid processes, and organizational silos place significant barriers in its path. Public service organizations and the siloes within the organizations are built for autonomy, not fluid, cross-boundary cooperation. Even when borders are crossed in good faith, conflicting cultures and work habits clash. Participants described divisive environments, low on trust, and high on impediments, characterized by issues such as over-complicated processes, poor access to information, and delayed support to those in need.

These issues did not cause participants to give up on collaboration through collective leadership, only to work harder to understand and overcome or work around the entrenched roadblocks inherent in the current public service model.

The Challenge of Wicked Issues

Resolving wicked problems requires time and space for creative thinking and working differently that the traditional structures and processes of public services do not offer (Lindblom 1979; Wilson 2002; Brewer and Walker 2010). The New Public Management (NPM) approach to public services introduced in the 1980s, with its emphasis on rationality and performance results, further inhibited any creative exploration. For participants, alternative ways of functioning and leading is required if the collaboration demanded by complex wicked problems is to be successful. The constant pressure to deliver and report back on collaborative work, for example, was cited as the kind of restrictive context that undermines efforts to effectively work together. More sophisticated approaches to measuring progress are needed for cross-organization collaborations.

Performance Measures

Measuring performance can no longer be conducted at the individual and organizational level. The focus, according to participants, must be on outcomes at the cross-boundary collective level. The broader context is vital not only for the effectiveness of the collaboration, but also for the motivation and morale of the people involved. Unfortunately, there is still much work to do. The dominant measurement evaluation system still places the emphasis on individual and organizational accountabilities and responsibilities. For public services to fulfill their mandate, performance measures must focus on improved outcomes for citizens, not on organizational interests and objectives.

Without a recalibration of performance measures, public services will continue to hamper efforts to address complex issues, work effectively across boundaries, and transform services. For example, collective leadership work, according to participants, should be evaluated based on long-term milestones and outcomes, not the short-term objectives of the past. And even when collective leadership produces short-term outcomes, such as process improvements, these outcomes should not be evaluated based on traditional measures, but on measures that focus on the growth realized from the accomplishment.

Collective leadership also requires performance measures that focus on the collaboration, not just the tasks. For example, performance evaluations would measure how well the group is working together. Progress on tasks is not ignored. Measuring task success, however, would include evaluating the impact of the collaborative process on task outcomes. For example, did the process alter how the group thought about or understood the problem?

The participants in this study, all experienced public service leaders, believe that meeting the needs of the public in the 21st century requires the 21st century approach to leadership, partnerships, public service structures and processes, problem-solving, and performance measurement offered by collaboration and collective leadership. The time for change is now.

CHAPTER 10

Conclusion: Advancing Collective Leadership

The collective leadership approach described in this book was presented in the context of public services in Scotland. Certainly, those interested in the work of the Collective Leadership for Scotland (CLS) and Project Lift initiatives, who informed the research at the core of the book in many different and invaluable ways, may wish to use this book to understand more about the aspects of their work – especially since the research is focused on the work that they did, accompanied by supporting theory, description, analysis, and visual interpretations.

That said, the applications of the lessons in this book extend far beyond public services in Scotland. Any organization that wishes to improve their collaborative practice, explore alternative conceptions of leadership, and understand or apply emergent versus planned approaches to change will find a blueprint for progress in these pages. Specifically, the book offers practice-based observations and guidance related to five key areas:

- **Attending to group process.** A recurring theme in this book is the importance of working on the collaborative process before attempting to work on the task.
- **Enriching conversations.** Being relational and having an inquiring approach lays the

foundation for problem-solving and the search for solutions. Sharing knowledge and ideas, listening attentively, being curious, and openness to changing your mind – all of these and more relational and dialogic practices prevent the group from jumping into solutions that are premature and ill thought out.
- **From planned to emergent.** An emergent process can be uncomfortable as it requires advancing into the unknown without a map. Yet eschewing the predetermined path, the emergent approach liberates the group to be creative and take risks, leading to new ideas and innovation
- **Joined-up working.** The breadth and complexity of issues and challenges with which organizations – in any sector – must deal with calls for a 'whole system' mindset that brings together all stakeholders to create a sustainable, shared way forward. Stakeholders will include citizens and communities for public organizations and customers and suppliers for traditional companies.
- **Productive reflection.** This book emphasizes deliberate, formal reflection on work practices (both individual and

collective). Improving how work gets done begins with sharing and thinking about experiences, values, and beliefs – our own and those of our collaborators. Traditionally, reflecting on improvement occurs periodically, for example at performance appraisal time. Here, time and space is given for the reflection to take place in real time, during the day-to-day work, which increases understanding and learning and leads to an enhanced practice.

Final Reflections

The experience of the participants in the real-world practice of collective leadership introduced a different perspective to the study of collaboration. Their experiences highlighted the importance of focusing on relationships and applying an emergent approach to lay the foundation for work on complex tasks. Task complexity also called for a systems-focused approach that involved multiple stakeholders from across all parts of the system. Diverse voices from other sectors, organizations, teams, and communities were welcomed into the collaboration.

A diverse group, however, can lead to divisions and competing interests and practices. Power imbalances can also occur. The collective

Conclusion: Advancing Collective Leadership

leadership approach, deliberately focused on learning and listening, working sensitively together, and understanding and accepting different perceptions and realities, allowed the participants' groups to work through differences.

The emergent principle placed the collaborative work in the context of a collective 'not knowing'. There were no predetermined best courses of action or solutions, only a shared acknowledgement that the issue was complex and no one organization or leader had the answer.

The collective leadership process was also built on productive, professional relationships that did not seek to avoid dissent or cover it up, since different points of view needed to be expressed and heard to ensure the best outcome of the collaboration.

Applying the four principles of collective leadership – systems, emergent, relational, and inquiry – to the real-world practice of an organization is no easy task. The capacity and skills required for collective leadership need to be developed. Facilitative support to help groups develop their collective leadership capability is essential to implement the principles and practices in this book. Facilitators can motivate, encourage, and manage the anxiety of those navigating the unknown and unfamiliar.

The observations, practices, and lessons of

this book will help leaders and companies think about new approaches to work-based learning, and the potential for the collaborative process under collective leadership. And although much emphasis is given to the collective, an important facet of successful collaboration and collective work is the importance of the individual's work on oneself. Personal reflection and self-awareness lead to an appreciation of why relationships come first and how power lies within the group and not above it.

In summary, to achieve the future of successful collaboration driven by collective leadership, we must be intentional in paying attention to how we work together more effectively in our own organizations and across organizational and sector boundaries.

Further Reading

1. Adams, W.C., 2015. Conducting semi-structured interviews. In: K.E. Newcomer, H.P. Hatry, and J.S. Wholey, eds. *Handbook of practical program evaluation*, pp. 492–505 San Francisco: Jossey-Bass.
2. Alvesson, M., Gabriel, Y. and Paulsen, R., 2017. *Return to meaning: a social science with something to say.* Oxford: Oxford University Press.
3. Ansell, C., Sørensen, E. and Torfing, J., 2020. The COVID-19 pandemic as a game changer for public administration and leadership? The need for robust governance responses to turbulent problems. *Public Management Review*, 23(7) pp.949-960.
4. Baggott, R., 2013. *Partnerships for public health and well-being: policy and practice.* Macmillan International Higher Education.
5. Barley, S.R., 2015. Confessions of a mad ethnographer. In: D. Elsbach and R. Kramer, ed. *Handbook of Qualitative Organizational Research: Innovative Pathways and Methods.* New York: Routledge, pp. 465-475.
6. Bolden, R., 2011. Distributed leadership in organizations: a review of theory and research. *International Journal of Management Reviews*, 13(3), pp. 251-269.
7. Braun, V. and Clarke, V., 2006. Using thematic analysis in psychology. *Qualitative Research in Psychology*, 3(2), pp. 77-101.
8. Brewer, G.A. and Walker, R.M., 2010. *The impact of red tape on governmental performance: an empirical analysis.* Oxford University Press.

9. Brookes, S. and Grint, K., eds. 2010. *The new public leadership challenge.* London: Springer Nature.
10. Bryman, A. and Burgess, B., 2002. *Analyzing qualitative data.* Routledge.
11. Cairney, P., 2017. Evidence–based best practice is more political than it looks: a case study of the 'Scottish Approach', *Evidence and Policy*, 13(3), pp.499-515.
12. Cairney, P., 2020.The Scottish Approach to Policymaking In: Michael Keating ed. *The Oxford Handbook of Scottish Politics.* Oxford University Press pp.464-480.
13. Carroll, B., Levy, L. and Richmond, D., 2008. Leadership as practice: challenging the competency paradigm. *Leadership,* 4(4), pp. 363-379
14. Christie, C., 2011. *Commission on the future delivery of public services.* Edinburgh: Scottish Government.
15. Collective Leadership, 2018. *How can we build capacity for collective leadership in Scotland?* [Online]. [Accessed on 22 June 2018]. Available from: https://collectiveleadershipscotland.com/wp-content/uploads/2019/03/how-can-we-build-capacity-for-collective-leadership-in-scotland.pdf
16. Connolly, J. and Pyper, R., 2020. In The leadership and management of public services reform in Scotland. In: Michael Keating ed. *The Oxford Handbook of Scottish Politics.* Oxford University Press pp.405-423.
17. Crosby, B.C. and Bryson, J.M., 2018. Why leadership of public leadership research matters: and

what to do about it. *Public Management Review*, 20(9), pp. 1265-1286.

18. Cullen-Lester, K.L. and Yammarino, F.J., 2016. Collective and network approaches to leadership: special issue introduction. *The Leadership Quarterly*, 27(2), pp. 173-180.

19. Currie, G., Grubnic, S. and Hodges, R., 2011. Leadership in public services networks: antecedents, process and outcome. *Public Administration*, 89(2), pp. 242- 264.

20. Dansereau, F.E. and Yammarino, F.J., 1998. *Leadership: The multiple-level approaches: Contemporary and alternative.* Elsevier Science/JAI Press.

21. Day, D.V., Gronn, P. and Salas, E., 2004. Leadership capacity in teams. *The Leadership Quarterly*, 15(6), pp. 857-880.

22. De Rivera, J. and Grinkis, C., 1986. Emotions as social relationships. *Motivation and Emotion*, 10(4), pp. 351-369.

23. Denis, J., Langley, A. and Rouleau, L., 2010. The practice of leadership in the messy world of organizations. *Leadership*, 6(1), pp. 67-88.

24. Dickinson, H. and Glasby, J., 2010. 'Why Partnership Working Doesn't Work' Pitfalls, problems and possibilities in English health and social care. *Public Management Review*, 12(6), pp. 811-828.

25. Dickinson, H. and Sullivan, H., 2013. Towards a general theory of collaborative performance: The importance of efficacy and agency. *Public Administration*, 92(1), pp. 161-177.

26. DiMaggio, P.J. and Powell, W.W., 1983. The iron cage revisited: institutional isomorphism and collective rationality in organizational fields. *American Sociological Review*, 48(2), pp. 147-160.
27. Dunleavy, P. and Hood, C., 1994. From old public administration to new public management. *Public Money & Management*, 14(3), pp. 9-16.
28. Fairhurst, G.T., Jackson, B., Foldy, E.G. and Ospina, S.M., 2020. Studying collective leadership: the road ahead. *Human Relations*, 73(4), pp. 598-614.
29. Friedrich, T.L., Vessey, W.B., Schuelke, M.J., Ruark, G.A. and Mumford, M.D., 2009. A framework for understanding collective leadership: the selective utilization of leader and team expertise within networks. *The Leadership Quarterly*, 20(6), pp. 933–958.
30. Gabriel, Y., 2000. *Storytelling in organizations: facts, fictions, and fantasies*. Oxford: OUP.
31. Gauthier, H., 2015. A multi-dimensional model for positive leadership. *Strategic Leadership Review*, 5(1), pp. 1-11.
32. Getha-Taylor, H., Holmes, M.H., Jacobson, W.S., Morse, R.S. and Sowa, J.E., 2011. Focusing the public leadership lens: research propositions and questions in the Minnowbrook tradition. *Journal of Public Administration Research and Theory*, 21(suppl_1), pp. i83-i97.
33. Goldsmith, S. and Eggers, W.D., 2005. *Governing by network: the new shape of the public sector*. Brookings Institution Press.

34. Heifetz, R.A. and Heifetz, R., 1994. *Leadership without easy answers.* Harvard University Press.
35. Helms, L., 2016. *Democracy and innovation: from institutions to agency and leadership.* Democratization, 23(3), pp. 459-477.
36. Herzog, H., 2012. Interview location and its social meaning. In: F. Jaber, J. A. Gubrium, A B Holstein, M McKinney and K D McKinney eds. *The SAGE handbook of interview research: the complexity of the craft.* SAGE, pp. 207-218.
37. Himmelman, A.T., 2001. On coalitions and the transformation of power relations: collaborative betterment and collaborative empowerment. *American Journal of Community Psychology*, 29(2), pp. 277.
38. Hood, C., 1991. A public management for all seasons? *Public Administration*, 69(1), pp. 3-19.
39. Hood, C., 1995. The "new public management" in the 1980s: variations on a theme. *Accounting, Organizations and Society*, 20(2), pp. 93-109.
40. Housden, P., 2014. This is us: a perspective on public services in Scotland. *Public Policy and Administration*, 29(1), pp. 64-74.
41. Isett, K.R., Head, B.W. and Vanlandingham, G., 2016. Caveat emptor: what do we know about public administration evidence and how do we know it? *Public Administration Review*, 76(1), pp. 20-23.
42. Joyce, P., 2004. Public sector strategic management: the changes required. *Strategic Change*, 13(3), p.107.

43. Joyce, P., 2021. Public governance, agility and pandemics: a case study of the UK response to COVID-19. *International Review of Administrative Sciences*, 87(3), pp536-555.
44. Kellis, D.S. and Ran, B., 2015. Effective leadership in managing NPM-based change in the public sector. *Journal of Organizational Change Management*, 28(4), pp. 614-626.
45. Koontz, T.M. and Thomas, C.W., 2006. What do we know and need to know about the environmental outcomes of collaborative management? *Public Administration Review*, 66, pp. 111-121.
46. Lincoln, Y.S. and Guba, E.G., 1985. *Naturalistic inquiry*. SAGE.
47. Lindblom, C.E., 1979. Still muddling, not yet through. *Public Administration Review*, 39(6), pp. 517-526.
48. Loeffler, E., Power, G., Bovaird, T. and Hine-Hughes, F., 2013. *Co-production of health and wellbeing in Scotland*. Birmingham: Governance International.
49. Lofland, J. and Lofland, L.H., 1995. Developing analysis. In: J. Lofland, D.A. Snow, L. Anderson and L.K. Lofland eds. *Analyzing social settings*, Wadsworth, pp. 183-203.
50. Lopez-Kidwell, V., Niven, K. and Labianca, G., 2018. *Predicting workplace relational dynamics using an affective model of relationships*. Journal of Organizational Behavior, 39(9), pp. 1129-1141.
51. Mackie, B., 2018. The Scottish Government's system of outcome-based performance management: a

case study of the National Performance Framework and Scotland Performs. In: E. Borgonovi, E. Anessi-Pessina and C. Bianchi eds, *Outcome-based performance management in the public sector.* Springer, pp. 81-105.

52. Marshall, C. and Rossman, G.B., 2014. *Designing qualitative research.* SAGE Publications.

53. Meijer, A.J., 2014. From hero-innovators to distributed heroism: an in-depth analysis of the role of individuals in public sector innovation. *Public Management Review*, 16(2), pp. 199-216.

54. Milner, E.M. and Joyce, P., 2005. *Lessons in leadership: meeting the challenges of public services management.* Psychology Press.

55. Morris, J., 1991. Minding our Ps and Qs. In: M. Pedlar, ed, *Action learning in practice*, 2nd edn, Brookfield, VT: Gower, pp. 71–80.

56. Oborn, E., Barrett, M. and Dawson, S., 2013. Distributed leadership in policy formulation: A sociomaterial perspective. *Organization Studies*, 34(2), pp. 253-276.

57. O'Connor, P.M. and Quinn, L., 2004. Organizational capacity for leadership. In: C. McCauley and E. Van Velsor eds. *The Center for Creative Leadership handbook of leadership development*, CA: Jossey-Bass, pp. 417-437.

58. O'Leary, R. and Vij, N., 2012. Collaborative public management: where have we been and where are we going? *The American Review of Public Administration*, 42(5), pp. 507-522.

59. Pedersen, D. and Hartley, J., 2008. The changing context of public leadership and management. *The International Journal of Public Sector Management*, 21(4), pp. 327-339.
60. Peräkylä, A., 1997. Conversation analysis: a new model of research in doctor– patient communication. *Journal of the Royal Society of Medicine*, 90(4), pp. 205-208.
61. Peters, B.G., 2011. Steering, rowing, drifting, or sinking? Changing patterns of governance. *Urban Research & Practice*, 4(1), pp. 5-12.
62. Pollitt, C., 1990. Doing business in the temple? Managers and quality assurance in the public services. *Public Administration*, 68(4), pp. 435-452.
63. Poocharoen, O. and Ting, B., 2015. Collaboration, co-production, networks: convergence of theories. *Public Management Review*, 17(4), pp. 587-614.
64. Potter, J. and Hepburn, A., 2012. Eight challenges for interview researchers. *Handbook of interview research*, 2(1), pp. 541-570.
65. Potter, J. and Wetherell, M., 1994. Analyzing discourse. In: B. Bryman and A. Burgess eds, *Analyzing qualitative data*. Routledge, pp. 47-66.
66. Raelin, J.A., 2003. *Creating leaderful organizations: how to bring out leadership in everyone.* Berrett-Koehler Publishers.
67. Raelin, J.A., 2017. Leadership-as-practice: theory and application – an editor's reflection. *Leadership*, 13(2), pp. 215-221.
68. Raelin, J.A., 2019. Deriving an affinity for collective leadership: below the surface of action learning.

Action Learning: Research and Practice, 16(2), pp. 123-135.

69. Ringer, T.M., 2007. Leadership for collective thinking in the workplace. *Team Performance Management: An International Journal*, 13(3/4), pp. 130-144.

70. Rubin, H. and Rubin, I., 1995. *Qualitative interviewing. The art of hearing data.* SAGE.

71. Salicru, S., 2020. A new model of leadership-as-practice development for consulting psychologists. *Consulting Psychology Journal: Practice and Research*, 72(2), p.79.

72. Schaefer, S.M. and Alvesson, M., 2020. Epistemic attitudes and source critique in qualitative research. *Journal of Management Inquiry*, 29(1), pp. 33-45.

73. Schein, E.H., 2013. *Humble Inquiry. The Gentle Art of Asking Instead of Telling.* Berrett-Koehler Publishers.

74. Scottish Government, 2011. *An introduction to Scotland's National Performance Framework.* Edinburgh, UK: The Scottish Government.

75. Scottish Government, 2018. *National Performance Framework.* Edinburgh, UK: The Scottish Government.

76. Seale, C. and Silverman, D., 1997. Ensuring rigour in qualitative research. *The European Journal of Public Health*, 7(4), pp. 379-384.

77. Selden, S.C., Sowa, J.E. and Sandfort, J., 2006. The impact of nonprofit collaboration in early childcare and education on management and program

outcomes. *Public Administration Review*, 66(3), pp. 412-425.

78. Senge, P., Hamilton, H. and Kania, J., 2015. The dawn of system leadership. *Stanford Social Innovation Review*, 13(1), pp. 27-33.

79. Senge, P.M., 2006. *The fifth discipline: the art and practice of the learning organization.* Currency.

80. Sharp, C., 2018. *Collective leadership: where nothing is clear and everything keeps changing. New Territories for Evaluation*, Workforce Scotland.

81. Silverman, D., 2019. What counts as qualitative research? Some cautionary comments. *Sotsiologicheskie Issledovaniya*, (8), pp. 44-51.

82. Silvia, C., 2018. Evaluating collaboration: The solution to one problem often causes another. *Public Administration Review*, 78(3), pp. 472-478.

83. Skelcher, C. and Sullivan, H., 2008. Theory-driven approaches to analysing collaborative performance. *Public Management Review*, 10(6), pp. 751-771.

84. Stiles, W.B., 1993. Quality control in qualitative research. *Clinical Psychology Review*, 13(6), pp. 593-618.

85. Stoker, G., 2006. Public value management: a new narrative for networked governance? *The American Review of Public Administration*, 36(1), pp. 41-57.

86. Thomson, A.M. and Perry, J.L., 2006. Collaboration processes: inside the black box. *Public Administration Review*, 66, pp. 20-32.

87. Torbert, W.R., 2004. *Action inquiry: The secret of timely and transforming leadership.* Berrett-Koehler Publishers.

88. Van Wart, M., 2013. Lessons from leadership theory and the contemporary challenges of leaders. *Public Administration Review*, 73(4), pp. 553-565.
89. Vangen, S. and Huxham, C., 2003. Nurturing collaborative relations: building trust in interorganizational collaboration. *The Journal of Applied Behavioral Science*, 39(1), pp. 5-31.
90. Watson, C., 2009. The 'impossible vanity': uses and abuses of empathy in qualitative inquiry. *Qualitative Research*, 9(1), pp. 105-117.
91. Wilson, J.L., 2002. Leadership development: working together to enhance collaboration. *Journal of Public Health Management and Practice*, 8(1), pp. 21-6.
92. Woolf, N.H. and Silver, C., 2017. *Qualitative analysis using NVivo: the five-level QDA® method*. Routledge.
93. Yin, R.K., 1994. Discovering the future of the case study. Method in evaluation research. *Evaluation Practice*, 15(3), pp. 283-290.
94. Yukl, G., 1999. An evaluation of conceptual weaknesses in transformational and charismatic leadership theories. *The Leadership Quarterly*, 10(2), pp. 285-305.

www.ingramcontent.com/pod-product-compliance
Lightning Source LLC
LaVergne TN
LVHW072023060526
838200LV00058B/4663